W9-DFC-635

DATE DUE

WHAT ARE THEY SAYING ABOUT THE TRINITY?

What Are They Saying About the Trinity?

by
Joseph A. Bracken, S.J.

PAULIST PRESS
New York/Ramsey/Toronto

Library of Congress
Catalog Card Number: 78-70819

ISBN: 0-8091-2179-4

Published by Paulist Press
Editorial Office: 1865 Broadway, New York, N.Y. 10023
Business Office: 545 Island Road, Ramsey, N.J. 07446

Printed and bound in the
United States of America

Contents

Preface

In beginning his book, *The Trinity*, Karl Rahner remarks: "Despite their orthodox confession of the Trinity, Christians are, in their practical life, almost mere 'monotheists.' "[1] Rahner goes on to add reasons, drawn from the history of theology, why the doctrine of the Trinity has received scant attention even from professional theologians. But the ordinary layperson can confirm from his/her own experience the truth in Rahner's statement: the Trinity is a matter of formal belief, but it has little or no resonance in day-to-day Christian life and worship. Part of the problem, of course, is a question of language. Most Christians refer to God as "He," and mean thereby sometimes the Father, sometimes the Son, sometimes the Spirit, but more often all of them in a generalized way and thus none of them specifically. Yet the reasons for this imprecision in theological language must lie deeper than simply the careless use of pronouns ("he" rather than "they"). Language, after all, reflects experience as well as shapes it; in all probability, we do not refer to God as "they" because we do not experience God as three distinct persons. Our experience is monotheistic rather than trinitarian.

In this connection, it is interesting to read

C. G. Jung's "A Psychological Approach to the Dogma of the Trinity."[2] Jung maintains that triads have been used to describe God or the divinity from the earliest times. He mentions, for example, the Babylonian triad of Anu, Bel and Ea; the Egyptian triad of Father, Son and Ka-mutef; and finally the cosmological speculations first of the Pythagorians and then of Plato in the Timaeus with respect to the number three. Jung concludes: "Arrangements in triads is an archetype in the history of religion, which in all probability formed the basis of the Christian Trinity."[3] If, however, a triadic concept of God is an archetypal reality in human consciousness, why has the dogma of the Trinity declined in the popular consciousness over the centuries of the Christian era? The answer may be partly found in Jung's further distinction between the logical idea of the Trinity and its psychological reality. The logical idea of the Trinity was first hammered out in the debates between rival theologians in the years prior to the Council of Nicaea; then the basic opposition between "person" and "nature," formulated by the Fathers at Nicaea, was given philosophical respectability by Thomas Aquinas and others after him, insofar as they defined a divine person to be a subsistent relation, a distinct way of being, within one and the same divine nature.[4] But the above solution to the logical problem of the Trinity may not have contributed to growth in the psychological reality of the Trinity among the faithful; quite the contrary, it may well have indirectly abetted its decline in significance for the faithful, since theological interest subsequently shifted to other areas of Christian belief (e.g., the divine-human character of the Redeemer), where a reasoned defense of orthodoxy was clearly needed.

In any case, it seems fair to say that for many years the dogma of the Trinity has been presented in manuals of theology more as a triumph of speculative reason than as a living article of Christian belief. Thus priests who with considerable effort learned the Thomistic explanation of the Trinity during their seminary years naturally hesitated to present it to their people from the pulpit, even on Trinity Sunday. Since there was no apparent pastoral value to be gained from an explanation of the doctrine, why should one bore people with something that in the end they wouldn't properly understand anyway? The net result, however, has been an informal conspiracy of silence among priests in pastoral work about the Trinity and the place of the dogma in Christian life and worship. Hence, more by inadvertence than anything else, Rahner's judgment that most Christians are practicing monotheists seems to me to have been verified in fact.

In recent years, however, there has been a new wave of interest in the doctrine of the Trinity both on the speculative and on the pastoral levels. With respect to the latter, the rapid multiplication of Charismatic Prayer groups among Christians of all persuasions gives testimony to a new presence of the Holy Spirit within the Church. Yet the operations of the Spirit cannot be understood apart from some knowledge of the Trinity. Hence, even on a strictly pastoral level, talk about the Trinity has taken on a new vitality and urgency. Likewise, within academic circles, the doctrine of the Trinity has come up for renewed consideration, if only because the classical synthesis of philosophy and theology worked out by Thomas Aquinas and his successors no longer is accepted without question. New ways of doing philosophy and theology have arisen which challenge not only the conclusions but, even more importantly, the theoretical presuppositions of the classical synthesis. The doctrine of the Trinity is thus just one of many traditional dogmas of the Church which in the past few years has undergone a searching re-examination.

In these pages I will attempt an overview of current theological reflection on the Trinity, beginning with those theories which are basically modifications of the classical doctrine, but then moving on to other theories which, as I noted above, seem to call into question the basic presuppositions of the traditional approach. Then, in the Epilogue, I will offer some personal reflections on what directions a new theology of the Trinity will presumably have to take, if it is to win and maintain the widespread acceptance which the older doctrine of the Trinity once enjoyed.

1
Updating of the Classical Doctrine

In this first chapter I will consider the theories of three Roman Catholic theologians who, in my opinion, have each presented an understanding of the Trinity which is indeed more relevant to contemporary thought patterns but which in its basic presuppositions still adheres to the classical explanation worked out by Thomas Aquinas in the *Summa Theologiae*. The first such theory is that of Bernard Lonergan in his two-volume work, *De Deo Trino*. In Part Two of that book, Lonergan has the following *Assertum*: "Father, Son and Holy Spirit are in virtue of one real consciousness three subjects conscious of themselves, of one another, and of their act [of being] both notional and essential."[5] This awareness both of themselves and of one another within the same act of consciousness would seem to guarantee to each of the three divine persons at least a minimal self-identity of personal consciousness. Difficulties arise, however, when one takes into account that the three divine persons, on the one hand, together constitute only a single conscious self in virtue of being one God and yet each of them, on the other hand, must have a distinctive self-identity, if they are to maintain their reality as separate persons. Lonergan says, for example, that God in virtue of his essential act of consciousness understands, knows and loves himself and others. Since Father, Son and Holy Spirit are equally God, each one of them understands, knows and loves himself and others by the same act of being. Yet the "self" which each of them thereby understands, knows and loves is not peculiar to any one divine person (for example, the Father) over the other two (the Son and the Holy Spirit), but rather is common to all three. Though they are three conscious subjects, they are nevertheless conscious of themselves as constituting a single self who understands, knows and loves himself perfectly. Admittedly, Lonergan puts the matter somewhat differently; he denies that the Father in virtue of the essential act of being has a distinct consciousness of the Son and the Spirit. Yet this seems to say indirectly what was affirmed above: namely, that the Father in virtue of the common consciousness has no awareness of himself (or his "self") as distinct from the common self which he shares with the Son and the Spirit.

So much for the divine consciousness as proper to the nature or essence and thus as common to all three persons. What is to be said of the same consciousness taken notionally, that is, insofar as each divine person shares in it differently? Lonergan claims that, in virtue of the processions and the real relations between the persons which arise there-from, the three divine persons each have an aware-ness of themselves and of one another as distinct individuals. By this he means that the Father con-sciously generates the Son and the Son is conscious of his generation by the Father. Both together are conscious of their common spiration of the Holy Spirit and the Spirit is conscious of his being spi-rated by the Father and the Son. Yet a closer exam-ination of these psychological relations between the divine persons reveals that the Father enjoys a de-cided pre-eminence over the Son and the Spirit in the matter of personal self-awareness and self-consciousness. For the Father not only knows and loves himself and others within the common con-sciousness, but notionally he is the one who active-ly generates the Son and spirates the Spirit. He is therefore even notionally a self within the divine nature, one who actively knows and loves. The same, however, is not true of the Son and the Spirit on the notional level. The Son is distinctive no-tionally as the *Verbum*, he who is known. It is true that he co-operates with the Father in the spiration of the Spirit and to this extent he too is a self, one who actively loves. But he is clearly less a self than the Father who both knows and loves. Finally, al-though the Holy Spirit is a knower and lover in virtue of the common consciousness, he is notion-ally considered not a self at all (in the sense of one who actively knows and loves). He is rather Love itself, that which passively proceeds from the act of loving exercised by another.

In brief, therefore, Lonergan's *Assertum*, quoted above, does not seem upon closer examination really to establish the distinct selfhood or self-consciousness of all three persons within the Trinity. Father, Son and Spirit are indeed three conscious subjects who share the same act of divine being or consciousness. Yet, in virtue of their common consciousness as one God, the three divine persons constitute only a single self who actively knows and loves himself and others. Moreover, insofar as they participate in this essential act of being individually, the three divine persons do not seem to be at all equal in the measure of their selfhood or self-awareness. Hence one seems obliged to conclude that the distinction of three conscious subjects within the Godhead only apparently solves the problem of the distinct selfhood or self-consciousness of all three divine persons. We are, of course, dealing here with divine mystery for which there is no completely satisfactory model or analogy. But it is, in any event, clear that Lonergan's explanation of the Trinity labors under roughly the same difficulties (from a pastoral point of view) as the classical theory: i.e., the remoteness of the concepts involved from practical experience; above all, the specialized understanding of "person," as applied to the members of the Trinity.

The second theologian to be considered in this

chapter is Karl Rahner. We have already taken note of his remark to the effect that Christians, although they profess a nominal belief in the Trinity, are practicing monotheists. The principal reason for this inconsistency between belief and practice, says Rahner, is the fact that the Trinity as such has not been intimately connected with salvation history. According to traditional Christian belief, any one of the three divine persons could have become man. Hence the relations of the persons to one another within the Godhead have no intrinsic bearing on the salvation of human beings. The doctrine of the Trinity can, accordingly, be treated more as an intellectual puzzle for the initiated than as a truth of vital importance for all Christians without exception.

Rahner himself, on the other hand, contends that only the Logos, the second person of the Trinity, could have become man, "because he is the Father's Word, in which the Father can express himself, and, freely, empty himself into the nondivine."[6] Likewise only the Spirit, the third person of the Trinity, could be given to man as the principle of uncreated love, hence of affective union between God and man, because he is already within the Trinity the affective bond between the Father and the Son. In brief, the "economic" Trinity (i.e., the Trinity as it manifests itself in creation and redemption) is the "immanent" Trinity and vice-versa. Otherwise, God cannot be said to communicate himself to man in and through creation and redemption:

God's self-communication is truly a *self-*communication. He does not merely give his creature some share of himself by creating and giving us created and finite realities through his omnipotent *efficient* causality. In a quasi-formal causality he really and in the strictest sense of the word bestows *himself*.[7]

Elaborating on this theme, Rahner suggests that there are two fundamental modalities in God's self-communication to human beings, namely, truth and love. In virtue of his truth (or, better, truthfulness), God reveals himself to men and women in history, making them an offer of friendship or intimacy. Then, in virtue of his love, God creates in human beings the ability to respond to his offer of friendship, thus opening to them a transcendent future, that which lies far beyond their normal hopes and desires. Yet in the thinking of the Church, truth and love have traditionally been identified with the Second and the Third Persons of the Trinity. Hence in the very concept of God's self-communication to mankind, the Persons of the Trinity stand revealed.

Impressive as this explanation of God's dealings with human beings surely is, there are still problems connected with Rahner's doctrine of the Trinity. For even though his understanding of the economic Trinity clearly reflects a heightened awareness of the strictly interpersonal relationships between God and man, Rahner hesitates to use the same interpersonal categories in his doctrine of the immanent Trinity. Throughout the book, but above all in its concluding pages, he calls into question the continued use by the Church of the term "person" to describe the reality of Father, Son and Holy Spirit as distinct from their nature as one God. He argues:

> When today we speak of person in the plural, we think almost necessarily, because of the modern meaning of the word, of several spiritual centres of activity, of several subjectivities and liberties. But there are not three of these in God—not only because in God there is only *one* essence, hence *one* absolute self-presence, but also because there is only *one* self-utterance of the Father, the Logos. The Logos is not the one who utters, but the one who is uttered. And there is properly no *mutual* love between Father and Son, for this would presuppose two acts.[8]

His own solution to the problem is to substitute the phrase "distinct manner of subsisting" for the word "person," so that he can state the mystery of the Trinity succinctly as follows: the one God subsists in three distinct manners of subsisting; the Father, Son and Spirit are the one God each in a different manner of subsisting and in this sense we may count "three" in God; God as subsisting in a determined manner of subsisting (such as the Father) is "somebody else" (*ein anderer*) than God subsisting in another manner of subsisting but he is not "something else" (*etwas anderes*).

The criticism that can be urged against Rahner here is then that, if interpersonal categories are used to illuminate the relations between God and human beings in the doctrine of the economic Trinity, then the same interpersonal categories should be employed in his exposition of the immanent Trinity. The term "person," therefore, as used to describe the distinct reality of Father, Son and Spirit within the immanent Trinity, cannot simply be abandoned without at the same time calling into question the real distinction of persons within the economic Trinity. If the one God subsists in three distinct manners of subsisting within the immanent Trinity, then he likewise subsists in the economic Trinity under three distinct modes or in three distinct manners. This would seem to be quite close to Sabellianism, i.e., the belief that the one God reveals himself under three different disguises or "masks." Rahner anticipates this objection to his theory and offers the following counter-argument:

Economic Sabellianism is false. . . . Such a conception of God's communication would basically be Arian, it would do away with a true *self*-communication of God. . . . It follows that this real mediation of a divine kind in the dimension of salvation history must also be a real mediation in God's inner life. The "threefoldness" of God's relation to us in Christ's order of grace is already the reality of God as it is in itself: a three-personal one.[9]

Taking Rahner at his word, however, one is led once again to question whether the term "person" can be abandoned in favor of "distinct manner of subsisting" without doing damage to the delicate balance between the economic and immanent Trinities. If Father, Son and Spirit are "persons" in the economic Trinity, then they should be "persons" within the immanent Trinity as well. Contrarily, if they are "distinct manners of subsisting" within the immanent Trinity, then they are likewise "distinct manners of subsisting" within the economic Trinity.

Rahner, of course, must regard as heretical any attempt by Christians to refer to the members of the immanent Trinity as separate "persons" because, as he says, "in God there is only one essence, hence one absolute self-presence."[10] Separate persons, on the other hand, would demand separate consciousnesses, numerically distinct psychological centers of operation. Accordingly, the members of the Trinity cannot be described as persons without destroying the unity of the divine essence. In this connection, his comments on the meaning and limits of the concepts of "person" and "nature" in the doctrine of the Trinity are very revealing. He begins with the supposition that "insofar as these concepts belong to the dogma of the Church, they intend to be only a logical, not an ontic explanation" of the doctrine of the Trinity.[11] He then takes advantage of this distinction to redefine the ontological meaning of the term "person" within the Trinity. "Person" in this context means "distinct manner of subsisting." He is not, however, quite so open to the possibility of revising the other key term, "nature" (or, as he uses it in this passage, "essence" or "substance"). "In principle," he says, "the concepts of essence and substance are not simply irreplaceable for the formulation of the trinitarian dogma. . . . Since they are but the "logical" explanation of the more primitive revelation, it is *a priori* not impossible that this kind of explanation may be presented also by means of other concepts."[12] Rahner himself, however, is at a loss as to what those "other concepts" could be.

To sum up, Rahner, like Lonergan, seems to be handicapped in his efforts at a new understanding of the Trinity by a highly specialized notion of the key term *person*. For, on the one hand, he is anxious to ground belief in the Trinity in the actual experience of Father, Son and Spirit within Christian life and worship; and, on the other hand, he is openly distrustful of the "tritheistic" overtones of that same day-to-day experience of the Trinity and seeks to remedy this defect by coining a new technical phrase, "distinct manner of subsisting," to substitute for the traditional word "person," at least with reference to the immanent Trinity. By this switch in terminology, however, Rahner seems implicitly to reaffirm what he ostensibly wished to change in virtue of his book: namely, the presumably too strong emphasis on God as one rather than as genuinely tripersonal in Christian life and worship. This is, of course, in no way to underestimate or demean the logic and speculative cogency of Rahner's exposition of the economic Trinity. But until the two "Trinities" can be better brought into harmony with one another, the doctrinal explanation of the Trinity remains perforce incomplete.

Still another Roman Catholic theologian who has written recently on the Trinity is Heribert Mühlen. In his book, *Der heilige Geist als Person*, Mühlen first takes note of the fact that the Holy Spirit in the classical understanding of the Trinity is not adequately understood as an individual person.[13] Aristotelian categories can be applied analogously to illuminate the act of divine generation, in virtue of which Father and Son exist as distinct persons; but these same categories are useless to render intelligible the act of spiration which is constitutive of the Holy Spirit as a person. Hence Mühlen concludes that only new categories drawn from the experience of interpersonal relations will suffice to illustrate the personal reality of the Holy Spirit. His solution is, in brief, to postulate that the Father is the subsistent I (*Ich*)-Relation, the Son the subsistent Thou (*Du*)-Relation, and the Holy Spirit the subsistent We (*Wir*)-Relation. In explanation of these new terms, Mühlen draws heavily both on the Trinitarian theology of the medieval scholastic Richard of St. Victor, and on the research of the nineteenth century German philosopher Wilhelm von Humboldt into the ontology of language.

Humboldt discovered in the course of his language studies that the personal pronouns I, Thou and He, together with their corresponding plural forms, are indispensable for the discourse-situation. The speaker invariably refers to himself as I, addresses his listener as Thou and speaks about a third party as He. From there he concluded that these personal pronouns are in reality relational concepts; that is, even though they refer to separate individuals, they are radically unintelligible except in reference to one another within the mind of the speaker. "Without a Thou, there is no I."[14] The speaker first understands himself as I, when he addresses another as Thou. Likewise, in referring to a third party as He or She, the speaker relates that person to the discourse-situation already created by the use of the pronouns I and Thou. Yet, insofar as the third party is not spoken to but only spoken about, the speaker implicitly reduces this other person to the level of an impersonal "object" of discourse. Hence the I-He (-She or -They) Relation must be regarded as an inferior mode of the fully personal I-Thou Relation.

Yet there is still another personal pronoun to be accounted for: namely, the "We" which the speaker employs, not to speak directly to another as Thou, but with another as an implicit acknowledgment of their antecedent union or community. To analyze the interpersonal relation signified by this pronoun,

Mühlen has recourse to the work of the German-American phenomenologist Dietrich von Hildebrand. In his *Metaphysik der Gemeinschaft,* von Hildebrand suggests that in the We-Relation two persons do not stand over and against one another, as in the I-Thou Relation, but rather next to one another and facing in the same direction.[15] Their union with one another is exhibited in their common stance over and against other people or in their working side-by-side to perform a given task. Mühlen himself develops this idea of von Hildebrand through reference to the process of human conception. Sexual intercourse is at one and the same time the perfection of the I-Thou Relation between a man and a woman and a striking instance of the We-Relation, if a given sexual act is productive of a child. Neither the man nor the woman alone could have produced the child, but only the two together in virtue of a common act were able to bring it into existence. In their common stance toward their child, therefore, they can say without hesitation: *We* are your parents; you are *our* child.

There are therefore three personal pronouns which grant a unique insight into the personhood or personal reality of the speaker: I, Thou, and We. Without a Thou, there can be no I; but without a Thou and I together, there can be no We. Mühlen's next task is to apply these insights from the ontology of language to the mystery of the Trinity in order to clarify the distinction of persons from one another. Here he openly admits his dependence on the Trinitarian theology of the medieval scholastic thinker Richard of St. Victor. Richard begins with the assumption that, since charity is the perfection of human nature, it must also be the perfection of the divine nature.[16] Yet this seems to demand by implication a plurality of persons within the Godhead. The love of God is infinite; hence no creature can be a worthy object of God's infinite love. On the other hand, without a plurality of persons within the divine nature, God could only love himself with an infinite love. This, however, is not the perfection of charity which consists rather in total self-donation to another. Hence one is brought logically to the conclusion that, if God is perfect charity, complete self-donation, then there must exist at least two persons within the Godhead who can love one another perfectly.

Richard then goes on to show that perfect charity demands the existence of not just two but, in fact, three persons. For, he argues, the love of two persons for one another would not yet be perfect, unless each was ready to share his/her love for the other with still a third person. The lover, in other words, not only loves his beloved as a second self but wishes that his beloved have the happiness of loving, and being loved by, still another person. His love for the beloved is so secure that he can tolerate without fear or jealousy a "rival" for the love of the beloved. If this degree of unselfishness is possible in human love, then it must *a fortiori* be operative within the divine nature. Hence perfect love within the Godhead demands the existence of not two but rather three persons. The Father first loves the Son as one truly worthy (*condignum*) of his infinite love. Both Father and Son then love the Spirit as one mutually loved (*condilectum*). The movement of love within the Trinity thus proceeds from self-love (the Father's love for himself), to mutual love (the Father's love for the Son and *vice-versa*), finally to "shared love" (the love of Father and Son together for the Spirit). Here love reaches its natural climax; hence the number of persons within the Godhead remains at three.

Given this context of strictly interpersonal relationships among the members of the Trinity and, above all, given this special understanding of the Holy Spirit as the one mutually loved (*condilectum*) by the Father and the Son, Mühlen is now in a position to develop his own theory for the distinction of persons within the Godhead. He suggests, as I noted earlier, that the Father is the subsistent I-Relation, the Son the subsistent Thou-Relation, and the Holy Spirit the subsistent We-Relation. In this way, each of the three divine persons corresponds to one of the three personal pronouns that give a unique insight into the personhood or personal reality of the speaker. As the personal pronouns are both distinct from and intimately related to one another in the mind of the speaker, so the three divine persons in virtue of these subsistent relations are both distinct from and related to one another within the unity of the divine nature. I will

now summarize Mühlen's argumentation in support
of that thesis, beginning with the hypothesis that the
Father is the subsistent I-Relation.

There is in God, Mühlen argues, only one consciousness, one self (*Selbst*), which is shared by the
Father, Son and Spirit in three distinct but related
ways. The Father as the subsistent I-Relation is
conscious of himself, first of all, as the *first* person,
that is, the one who is underived, without origin
from another. Just as the I is the logical antecedent
of the Thou within the I-Thou Relation, so the first
characteristic of the Father as the subsistent
I-Relation is to be the Unoriginated, the first person. But the Father is likewise he who generates the
Son. Here too the notion of the Father as the subsistent I-Relation is right to the point. Without a Thou,
no I. Without the Son to address as Thou, the
Father would not be in the full sense of the word an
I. The Father as the subsistent I-Relation is likewise
he who with the Son says "We" and thereby spirates the Spirit, but we will postpone this consideration for a moment in order to concentrate on the
Son as the subsistent Thou-Relation.

In his analysis of the Son as the subsistent
Thou-Relation, Mühlen leans heavily on the Trinitarian theology of Richard of St. Victor, explained
above, as well as on St. Thomas's doctrine of the
Trinity in the *Summa Theologiae*. He notes, first of
all, that the Son as the divine Word is not only the
Word that is known but also the Word that is loved
by the Father. Hence the Word must be another

person who can return the Father's love and thus be a worthy "object" or recipient of the Father's unbounded love. Second, Mühlen notes that the Thou in a conversation is that person from whom the I expects an answer or a response. For both these reasons, the Son is, in Mühlen's opinion, best described as the subsistent Thou-Relation. He is the partner of the Father in the dialogue of divine love: he to whom the Father says, Thou, and from whom the Father expects a loving response. As the subsistent Thou-Relation, however, the Son is strictly speaking not an I. Within their I-Thou Relation, only the Father is I; the Son is always Thou. Hence his response to the Father is that of Thou to Thou (*Du-Du*), not of I to Thou. This difficulty with the strict application of interpersonal categories to the members of the Trinity will be considered more in detail later, when I offer a critique of Mühlen's theory as a whole. First, however, Mühlen's understanding of the Holy Spirit as the subsistent We-Relation must be considered.

Mühlen initially takes note of the fact that at the Second Council of Lyons and again at the Council of Florence the assembled bishops affirmed that the Holy Spirit proceeds eternally from the Father and the Son, not as two principles or sources of activity, but as one principle or source of activity; not in virtue of two spirations, but in virtue of a single spiration. In his *Summa Theologiae*, Thomas Aquinas had already made the same point in somewhat more nuanced theological language: although there are two distinct persons, namely the Father and the Son, who spirate the Spirit (*duo spirantes*), they are not by that fact two spirators (*duo spiratores*), but rather together a single spirator.[17] Since the activity of spiration is proper to the one divine nature rather than to the persons as such, Father and Son operate as a single principle in breathing forth the Spirit. Mühlen then suggests that this unique conjunction of the two divine persons in one and the same essential operation is a perfect instance of the We-Relation described above. That is, Father and Son in virtue of the activity of spiration can say equivalently to the Spirit: *We* are your spirator; you are *our* Spirit. The Spirit, in turn, not only emanates from the We-Relation of the Father and the Son, but is himself the hypostatized We-Relation. In this respect the We-Relation between Father and Son is different from the We-Relation existing between a husband and wife in the generation of a child. Whereas the child after generation has his own being distinct from that of his parents, the Spirit has no being apart from the We-Relation existing between Father and Son. His personhood or self-identity consists in being their ongoing We-Relation, itself "become" another person. Looked at from the viewpoint of the traditional doctrine of perichoresis, the Spirit is one person "in" two persons. That is, whereas the Father and the Son are "in" one another because of their mutual I-Thou Relation, the Spirit is "in" both Father and Son at the same time, because he is their We-Relation.

Mühlen freely admits that there are problems connected with this understanding of the Holy Spirit as the subsistent We-Relation. How does the Spirit, for example, address the Father and the Son? He must, according to Mühlen, address them together as You in the plural (German *Ihr*). They can address him as Thou (*Du*), but he can speak to them only as a pair, never as individuals. Furthermore, even to address Father and Son as You in the plural, the Spirit must be in some sense an I. His being the subsistent We-Relation between the Father and the Son would not seem to equip him *ipso facto* to respond to their mutual Thou. Mühlen had, of course, the same problem with the Son as the subsistent Thou-Relation. In that instance, however, he insisted that the relation between the Son and the Father was Thou-Thou (*Du-Du*), not I-Thou. To be fully consistent, he should have labeled the Spirit's relation to the Father and the Son together as We-You (plural), instead of I-You (plural). Or he should have conceded that the Son as the subsistent Thou-Relation is still in some sense an I.

Upon closer examination it is clear that Mühlen's difficulties with the strict application of interpersonal categories to the members of the Trinity is due to his assumption that there is only one consciousness or self (*Selbst*) within the Trinity.[18] Hence, even though the members are related to one another on an interpersonal basis, only the Father as the subsistent I-Relation seems to be closely associated with the self of the divine nature. He alone is able to relate to the other two persons on an interpersonal basis without some resultant ambiguity. Mühlen, of course, feels obliged to maintain this ambiguity, however undesirable in itself, because of the danger of tritheism, i.e., belief in three gods. As he sees it, three I's, that is, three independent centers of consciousness within the Godhead, could not be reconciled with the unity of nature required by belief in one God.

Hence one sees that with Mühlen too the stumbling block to a more genuinely interpersonal explanation of the relations of the Father, Son and Spirit with one another is paradoxically the notion of person. What we human beings understand by person, namely, an independent center of consciousness capable of rational choices, is just not applicable to the Trinity without the concomitant danger of tritheism. On the other hand, Rahner's remarks, quoted above, to the effect that "person" and "nature" are logical rather than strictly ontological categories, hence that they "are not simply irreplaceable for the formulation of the trinitarian dogma," would lead one to wonder whether further reflection on the traditional understanding of the divine "nature" might not be the next logical step in trying to work out a new concept of the Trinity. As a matter of fact, all the writers in the next two chapters have done precisely that; i.e., they have all from quite different perspectives sought to redefine the nature or essence of God.

2
New Approaches to the Trinity: I

While it might seem at first blush strange to call into question the "nature" or "essence" of God, one should always remember that we are dealing here with a philosophical understanding of God, which is finite and therefore subject to change, rather than with the actual reality of God, which surpasses all human efforts to comprehend it and which basically always has been and always will be whatever it is here and now. Ludwig Fuerbach failed to make this distinction when he suggested that God is made in the image and likeness of man. There is, of course, a half-truth here; human understanding of God is directly linked to the collective self-understanding which human beings have of themselves in any given age of the world. When that self-understanding changes, then one can anticipate a corresponding change in the contemporary understanding of God. But the reality of God, as something fundamentally independent of our efforts to understand it, remains forever whatever it actually is.

Keeping this in mind, we can better understand

what Jürgen Moltmann is trying to accomplish in his recent book *The Crucified God*, when he says: "The cross stands at the heart of the trinitarian being of God; it divides and conjoins the persons in their relationships to each other and portrays them in a specific way. . . . From the life of these three, which has within it the death of Jesus, there then emerges who God is and what his Godhead means."[19] But the concept of God which thus emerges is substantially different from that worked out at Nicaea and the other early councils of the Church. At Nicaea and again at the first council of Constantinople, for example, the Church fathers declared that Jesus Christ as the Son of God was begotten, not made, one in being with the Father. Hence, like the Father, he is immutable and unchangeable in his divine nature. In his human nature, to be sure, he was born of the Virgin Mary, suffered the ordinary pains of human existence, and eventually died on the cross. Furthermore, in virtue of the doctrine of the communication of idioms, one can say that all this happened to the Son of God, but only "in the flesh," i.e., in his conjoined human nature. The divine nature as such, which he shares with the Father and the Spirit, must remain thereby unaffected. As Moltmann suggests, this was a quite deliberate attempt on the part of the Church fathers to bring the Christian understanding of the Trinity into line with the best philosophical thought on the nature of God in the ancient world. That is, from the time of Plato and Aristotle it was taken for granted in philosophical circles that God or the Supreme Being, in contrast to the finite creatures of this world, must be eternal and unchanging, incapable of being affected either negatively or positively by events in this world. The Stoic ideal of *apatheia*, complete control of the passions, was thus transferred in an idealized form to the inner life of God, so that neither creation as a whole nor any part of it, i.e., the fate of individual human beings, could disturb the harmony and tranquility of life within the Godhead.

What Moltmann has in mind, of course, is something entirely different. According to his theory, the entire Trinity is deeply involved in the death of Jesus on the cross. Taking as his starting-point Romans 8:31 ("If God is for us, who is against us? He who did not spare his own Son but gave him up for us all, will he not also give us all things with him?"), Moltmann argues that the Father grieves over the death of his Son: "The Son suffers dying, the Father suffers the death of the Son. The grief of the Father here is just as important as the death of the Son."[20] In effect, Jesus on the cross experiences the agony of being temporarily forsaken by the Father, while the Father in the same moment experiences the anguish of being separated from his Son, hence of losing his own identity as Father. Yet, says Moltmann, in this surrender of their mutual identity as Father and Son for the sake of sinful human beings, Jesus and the Father experience a new unity with one another in the Spirit. The Spirit, in other words, precisely as the personification of self-giving love, re-establishes the community between Father and Son in the very moment that they are prepared to renounce it for the sake of their sinful creatures. Furthermore, the Spirit is thereby set loose in the world to reconcile men and women with their God and to set up the conditions for a deeper and richer form of human life. For it is now obvious that nothing in human life, not even death itself, can separate us from the love of God the Father, revealed to us in the death of his Son on the cross.

Important for our purposes in this essay is Moltmann's insistence that the dramatic events on Calvary cannot be properly understood and evaluated except in terms of an explicit belief in the Trinity. Karl Barth in his *Church Dogmatics*, for example, had earlier insisted that God suffered rejection at the hands of men in the death of Jesus on the cross.[21] But, argues Moltmann, who is God in this instance except the eternal Father? Furthermore, unless it be specifically stated that the Father likewise suffered in the death of his Son, then it is not immediately clear that the passion, death and resurrection of Jesus is an event which took place within God as well as to one of the divine persons in his human nature. The three divine persons, in other words, must truly participate in all the pain and suffering of human history, make human history in effect part of their own divine life, if they are genuinely to effect the redemption of the world. As Moltmann comments, "only if all disaster, forsakenness by God, absolute death, the infinite curse of damnation and sinking into nothingness is in God himself, is community with this God eternal salvation, infinite joy, indestructible election and divine life. The 'bifurcation' in God must contain the whole uproar of history within itself."[22]

The God of classical theism, whether conceived as a Trinity of persons or simply as one God, was by definition an *absolute* being, impervious to all human pain and suffering, at least in his (their) own internal life and activity. Reflective human beings, accordingly, unable to cope with God's apparent impassivity in the face of human pain and suffering, chose rather to be atheists, to believe that there was no God, than to admit that God did not care enough to share the pain and suffering with them and thus to offer them the hope of eventual redemption. The task of Christian theology, as Moltmann sees it, is to overcome the classical opposition between theism and atheism with a purified understanding of the passion, death and resurrection of Jesus as an inner-trinitarian event. As he notes, "the God of theism is poor. He cannot love nor can he suffer."[23] The Father of Jesus Christ, however, suffers the loss of his Son (and his own fatherhood) in the death of Jesus on the cross. Thereby he suffers the "contradiction" of great evil without angrily seeking revenge on his rational creatures. The Son too suffers the pain of Godforsakenness and eventually of death itself, so that he will forever after be in a position to console those human beings who suffer a similar plight. Finally, the Spirit is involved, first to reconcile Father and Son to one another in the very act of self-giving love and then to communicate to human beings the same inner-trinitarian life, i.e., the power to overcome evil through self-giving love, suffering love.

What is distinctive about Moltmann's presentation here is the artful way in which he combines the traditional doctrine of the Trinity, above all, as interpreted by Karl Barth, with the perspectives of Alfred North Whitehead and other process thinkers on the nature of God. To be specific, Karl Barth speaks movingly of God's willingness to endure the consequences of sin in order to redeem his rational creatures. But all this is done in the person of his Son, Jesus Christ, who in his human nature suffered the psychological pain of rejection, the physical sufferings of the crucifixion, etc. Within the inner life of the Trinity, none of this pain and suffering is to be found. There the three divine persons enjoy the blessedness which has been theirs from all eternity. Alfred North Whitehead and the other process thinkers, on the other hand, quite willingly concede that God is really affected by the events taking place within creation, but by and large they do not think of God in specifically trinitarian terms. They are, in other words, monotheists who think of God and the world as complimentary realities within a single comprehensive process.

As Whitehead notes in *Process and Reality*, "God is the infinite ground of all mentality, the unity of vision seeking physical multiplicity. The World is the multiplicity of finites, actualities seeking a perfected unity."[24] Evil, accordingly, is present in God because it is concomitantly present in the world. At the same time, evil in this world is not an ultimate reality; it has already been transformed into good by reason of its inclusion within the nature of God. That is, God saves the world from potential self-destruction, in that everything evil (as well as everything good) eventually finds its place within the objective unity of all things which is God's "consequent nature." "Every fact is what it is, a fact of pleasure, of joy, of pain, or of suffering."[25] But in its inclusion within the nature of God, it becomes part of a broader scheme of things which is ultimately good.

For Whitehead, of course, God is personal without being tripersonal. That is, he does not envision a community of three persons who together constitute one God. Within his scheme of things, God is the one "actual entity" who "prehends" all the other actual entities and thus gives a unity and direction to the world process which it otherwise would not have. In fact, it would be a contradiction of his basic metaphysical presuppositions if God were conceived as a Trinity. For then every other actual entity would likewise have to have a triune structure. God, in other words, is for Whitehead the supreme exemplification of what is meant by an actual entity. What holds true for God must likewise apply to every other actual entity in the universe, even the smallest unit of energy.

Likewise, theologians who have used Whitehead's philosophy to work out a new understanding of creation, grace, eschatology, etc., have for the most part not been explicitly Trinitarian thinkers. Charles Hartshorne, for example, speaks of God as social; but by that he means that God is really related to his creatures by bonds of love and sympathy, hence that he is not the impassible Absolute of traditional metaphysics. Furthermore, neither John Cobb, David Griffin nor Schubert Ogden appear to conceive God in terms of a community of three divine persons; for each of them God is eminently personal, but not tripersonal. Norman Pittenger, to be sure, refers to God as "The Three in One," but he sees difficulties in applying the term "person" in the modern psychological sense to the members of the Trinity. Similarly, Lewis Ford, in an article entitled "Process Trinitarianism," suggests that there is a triunity of principles within God: namely, the non-temporal creative act of God, its outcome within his primordial nature, and the divine experience of the world as his consequent nature. Moreover, these three principles can be respectively related to the "Father," the "Son" and the "Holy Spirit" of traditional Christian belief. But, says Ford, this does not imply "a plurality of subjects in personal interaction within the Godhead."[26] For once again "person," in the accepted contemporary meaning of the term, seems to imply three independent centers of consciousness, hence three Gods, not one God.

Moltmann, however, as noted above, manages to combine traditional belief in the Trinity with a notion of God as process. Is his merger of these two traditions really successful or only apparent? What struck me on reading the book is that Moltmann has not provided an underlying conceptual framework within which to integrate the two traditions. That is, he merely states that the Father grieves over the death of his Son and that the Son experiences abandonment by his Father on the cross. He does not go on to show how the reality of three distinct persons is possible within a process-approach to God. Similarly, he merely states that human history is taken up into the inner life of God and thus becomes part of the "history" of the Trinity itself. But he does not make clear, from a systematic point of view, how this is possible without sacrificing either divine transcendence or human freedom. What is needed, in other words, is a thoroughgoing process approach which begins with the premise that God is a community of three divine persons and then proceeds to show how this triune life of God is somehow continued in the process of creation as a whole but above all in the lives of human beings redeemed by Jesus. Short of this broad systematic development, Moltmann's scheme, however provocative it might be in itself, seems to remain more at the level of pious metaphor than established hypothesis.

Other theologians, however, have been at work on this same problem; and their efforts, though likewise tentative and incomplete, shed light on the full metaphysical system that will eventually have to be worked out, if this new line of thought about the inner life of God is to win the confidence of reflective Christians. The first such theologian is the American process thinker, Daniel Day Williams, above all in his book, *The Spirit and Forms of Love*. A second is the German theologian, Heribert Mühlen, whose work on the Trinity we have to some extent already analyzed and critiqued in these pages. For, subsequent to the publication of *Der heilige Geist als Person*, Mühlen put out a second work in which he offers a new concept of God's nature or essence. Much in line with Moltmann's thought on the subject, it deserves consideration here because of its more scholarly approach to these same issues.

As Williams sees it, the biblical affirmation that God is love (1 Jn. 4:16) has never been explored in its fullness because of the reluctance of scholastic philosophers and theologians to describe the nature of God in frankly anthropomorphic terms. Yet the result has been a negative theology of God which more resembles the Supreme Being of Greek metaphysics than Jahweh in the Hebrew Bible or the Father of our Lord Jesus Christ in the Christian dispensation. Accordingly, in *The Spirit and Forms of Love*, Williams first undertakes a phenomenological analysis of human love and then applies the categories therein discovered to an understanding of God as revealed in the Bible as a whole, but above all in the person of Jesus. The first category, says Williams, is that of individuality. Only real individuals, unique beings, can truly love one another. Love in fact heightens individuality, since each helps the other to become more perfectly him/herself. Applied to God, this means that God must be personal; furthermore, he must be in vital contact with his creatures. For "an absolutely solitary individual can neither love nor be loved."[27] Descriptions of God as the Ground of Being or Being itself, therefore, are basically inconsistent with the Biblical affirmation that God is love, hence an utterly personal being capable of communion with other persons.

The second category pertaining to human love is freedom: both our own freedom to love another and the freedom of the other to love us in return. That which is coerced in any way cannot be love. Applied to God, this means that God in loving us must risk a refusal on our part to love him. If he persists in loving us even though we fail to love him as we should, then God in some sense "suffers" in his love for us, as the third category of love, action and suffering, makes clear. To love, says Williams, is to act, to exert influence upon another in the exercise of his/her freedom. But it also implies being acted upon, "suffering" the influence of another for good or for ill in one's own person. Impassibility makes love meaningless. Applied to God, this means that God suffers with his creatures in their trials and sorrows, precisely because he loves them. Admittedly, this does not mean that God suffers in exactly the same way as human beings do. God is not threatened in the integrity of his being by suffering. He can bear suffering so much better than human beings because he sees the total picture in which this particular suffering has meaning both for the individual and for the race as a whole. But this is nevertheless not to deny that God as a compassionate Father suffers with his children in their faltering attempts to love one another and himself.

The fourth category, causality, is basically a further precision of the second and the third. It proposes that human beings in their mutual love exercise a special type of causality on one another; i.e., they *motivate* each other to make decisions favorable to the future of their relationship together. Yet it is a causality which respects the basic freedom of the other party to choose otherwise, to make decisions opposed to the continuance of the relationship. Applied to God, this means that God's grace can never be overpowering in its effects on human free will. God persuades us to respond to his loving initiative, much as a lover persuades his/her beloved to pursue a course of action favorable to the maintenance and growth of the relationship. But this once again implies that God is deeply involved with his rational creatures, suffering with them in their doubts and hesitations about what to do and whom to love deeply. The fifth and last category, says Williams, is impartial judgment in loving concern for the other: "to love is to accept responsibility for assessing the real situation in which we love, and that means self-discovery and discovery of the other."[28] True love, in other words, is never blind; passionate desire may not overrule the dictates of justice, either with respect to the beloved or vis-à-vis some third party likewise involved in the relationship. The application to God is evident. God alone is in a position to judge with perfect impartiality, since he knows each of us perfectly and genuinely seeks only what is for our greater good.

Thus far in his analysis of the Scriptural saying that God is love, Williams has referred to God persistently in the singular, with only a hint here and there that perhaps God is a community of persons who first love one another and then, out of the fullness of their love for one another, create rational creatures to share in that love. But in his application of this process-understanding of God to the Christian doctrines of the Incarnation and the atonement, Williams reveals more clearly the Trinitarian basis of his thought. In discussing the meaning of the Incarnation, for example, he remarks: "The union of God and man in Jesus Christ is the communion of God with the man Jesus. It is a communion in which the deity of God and the humanity of Jesus are joined in the freedom of love. God in his grace created a humanity which becomes responsive to him and committed utterly to him."[29] Admittedly, Williams' language here is adoptionist; i.e., his words seem to imply that Jesus was first a man who then became the Son of God as a result of a lifelong submission to the will of the Father. But, as Williams shrewdly notes, to speak of two natures in Christ, one divine and the other human, is implicitly to admit that Jesus only experienced "the risks, dilemmas and decisions of a real human being" in his human nature, that in his divine nature, on the contrary, he remained curiously impassive to all that went on about him during his earthly life. Williams, accordingly, prefers to use adoptionist language with its resultant ambiguities for the traditional doctrine of the Incarnation, in order to emphasize that in Jesus God really became man, that he shared with his creatures in their day-to-day trials and sufferings, and finally that he enjoyed a certain freedom and independence vis-à-vis the Father, so as to be able to respond freely to the latter's grace. Only thus is the Incarnation living proof that God, as noted above, accepts human beings with their freedom of choice and through his grace enables them to grow in that same freedom.

Reflecting on the sufferings of Jesus during his earthly life, but above all on the cross, Williams then asks himself whether the Father likewise suffered with Jesus. His answer is: "How can we speak of love between Father and Son if the Father is unmoved by the Son's suffering?"[30] Once again, Williams is attacking the traditional understanding of God as impassible, unable to be moved by the actions of his creatures. Pointing to the "Tome of Leo" which served as the model for the doctrine of the two natures in Christ enunciated at the Council of Chalcedon, he notes that Pope Leo attributes the miracles of Jesus to his divinity and his suffering, hunger and thirst to his humanity. Thus power is seen as a divine attribute, suffering as a human weakness. Quite the contrary, says Williams, is not suffering for and with others a much more significant revelation of what it means to be God than the mere suspension of the laws of nature? Human beings, to be sure, seek to be like "God" in the exercise of power and dominion over their fellow human beings. But this craving for power is likewise the root of sin in human life. It would be far better for us genuinely to imitate the divinity through sharing with others in their trials and sufferings, showing compassion, rather than seeking to dominate and control.

In still another passage, Williams points out that suffering is a necessary precondition for deeper communication between persons in this life. "The deepest discovery in love is that the other suffers for us, and we discover that we love when we suffer for and with the other."[31] Admittedly, not all suffering is constructive; suffering can be self-destructive to the point of shattering any hope of finding a meaning in existence. But in the suffering of Jesus during his earthly life and above all on the cross, there is revealed the Father's loving will simultaneously to oppose the evils everywhere present in human life and yet to seek the reconciliation of men and women with himself and one another. As Williams remarks, Jesus had first to oppose human iniquity in all its ugliness before he could openly offer to his contemporaries the Father's love and forgiveness. Simply to announce the forgiveness of sin without doing anything to effect a conversion of heart among his hearers would only trivialize God's love and man's sin. Inevitably, however, this course of action led to a painful confrontation with his enemies and ultimately to his death on the cross as a condemned criminal. Yet, from beginning to end, Jesus never gave up the effort to communicate with his fellow human beings, even using his passion and death as a final testimonial to the seriousness of his message. It was rather the Scribes and Pharisees and their followers who could no longer "suffer" the effects of Jesus' words on themselves and sought to terminate this "suffering" by putting him to death. In a striking way, therefore, the history of the passion verifies Williams' basic thesis that all deeper communication between persons (at least in this life) involves suffering, a condition from which even the three divine persons in their dealings with us are not exempt.

The notion that God is capable of suffering for his creatures must be surely bizarre for many people. Perhaps for this very reason, Williams is quite cautious and deliberate in making such statements. He says, for example: "God does not surrender his deity, his everlastingness, the perfection of his power and love. God remains God. But if God is love he does his creative and redemptive work by involving himself in the history of human freedom with its tragedy. God's deity is manifest supremely at the very point where Leo sees only humanity, that is in the weakness, suffering, and dying of Jesus."[32] In still another place, he argues that, while suffering may threaten the being and integrity of human beings because of their relative inability to deal with it objectively, it never threatens the being and integrity of God. God's higher purposes in creation are accomplished, not only in spite of the pain and suffering in the world, but somehow in and through this same pain and suffering. Yet, in permitting such suffering, the three divine persons are themselves personally affected.

Referring to his earlier statement that the Father is profoundly moved by the sufferings of his Son on the cross, Williams notes that to say the opposite, namely, that the Father is unmoved by the sufferings of his Son, leads to the conclusion that the sufferings of Jesus are somehow the price to be paid for the forgiveness of our sins. Not the love of God, but rather the all-too-human vindictiveness of God is then revealed in the drama on Calvary. Accordingly, it seems far better to admit that God too suffers in his love for us. For "if God does not suffer then his love is separated completely from the profoundest human experiences of love, and the suffering of Jesus is unintelligible as the communication of God's love to man."[33] Finally, and from a philosophical point of view perhaps most importantly, Williams calls attention to the fact that the traditional understanding of God as impassible is rooted in a Neo-Platonic notion of Being which may or may not be appropriate to a contemporary understanding of God. That is, according to Plato and his followers down the centuries, the world of Being, namely, the world of unchanging forms and ideas, is superior to the world of Becoming, where these eternal forms are temporarily incarnated. Hence God as the single perfect being must dwell in the world of Being rather than be subject to the contingencies of the world of Becoming. But it is precisely this philosophical presupposition, i.e., the priority over Being over Becoming, which Williams and other process thinkers directly challenge. In their view, Becoming enjoys a priority over Being; Being at any given moment is only a stage in the total process of Becoming. Hence, more than any of his creatures, God suffers, precisely because he is most completely involved in the process of Becoming.

There are, of course, still problems connected with Williams' hypothesis. He leaves unanswered, for example, the question whether and how God exercises providence over his creation. Does the suffering of God, in other words, imply that God is finite, i.e., that he cannot alter or perhaps ever foresee the direction which the process of creation will take in the future? Whitehead in *Process and Reality* argues that God uses persuasion rather than force in dealing with his creatures. But this implies that God does not know what his creatures will do until they actually do it. In his "primordial nature," to be sure, God envisages all the structures of possibility that exist for this world, and it is in the light of these possibilities that God makes suggestions (proposes "initial aims") to his creatures. But, strictly speaking, God does not know which of these structures of possibility will be actualized in any given case until it actually happens. Hence, in his "consequent nature" God is as dependent upon the world process, as the world process is dependent upon him in his primordial nature for its own sense of purpose and direction.[34] What remains unanswered in Williams' treatment of God, therefore, is whether he too like Whitehead endorses the concept of a finite God as a necessary consequence of the belief in God's capacity to suffer, or whether he foresees some way to "save" God's infinity, i.e., the traditional understanding of his omnipotence and omniscience, even as he continues to affirm that God also suffers.

Despite these ambiguities in his presentation, there seems to be a ring of truth in Williams' persistent affirmation that suffering in some sense is a factor in genuine love, hence that Jesus' revelation of the Father in his life and, above all, in his death on the cross, is the revelation of One who cares for his creatures, even to the point of suffering on their behalf. Moreover, basically the same point is made by Heribert Mühlen in his work referred to above, *Die Veränderlichkeit Gottes als Horizont einer zukünftigen Christologie.*[35] Mühlen, to be sure, even more than Williams, presents his new under-

standing of God in conscious opposition to the received doctrine enunciated at Nicaea, First Constantinople and Chalcedon. But for that same reason, his presentation deserves careful attention,
since he clearly has in mind to mediate between the
old and the new in the matter of our human understanding of God.

Mühlen begins by taking note of the altered
world-consciousness of human beings in this century. The universe is no longer conceived as an impersonal Whole, but rather as an interpersonal We.
Being is primarily understood in terms of human
beings and their interrelations with one another.
Man is no longer a part of nature, but nature is a
part of man's world, something to be transformed
through human technology. Changes, accordingly,
are needed in the traditional concepts of God the
Father and his Son Jesus Christ, if Christianity is to
keep pace with this altered self-image of the human
race. But these changes must be made, as far as
possible, in line with the basic intention of the
Church Fathers, above all at the Council of Nicaea,
when they worked out the classical terminology to
describe the relation between the Father and the
Son. A careful study of pertinent conciliar texts together with the commentaries of Eusebius and
Athanasius reveals, for example, that the Fathers at
Nicaea meant by the term *homoousios* only to affirm   that   Jesus   was   of   the   same   being
(*gleichseiendlich*) with the Father.[36] They did not
further specify what the being or nature of God in

itself is. Admittedly, they may have thought in terms of a single indivisible divine substance, which cannot in any way be divided between Father and Son. But their explicit affirmations at Nicaea were limited to a denial of the Arian heresy, namely, that Jesus was God, of equal stature with the Father, and therefore not a creature.

The issue of the underlying nature or inner reality of God, however, was inevitably at stake in the Father's discussion of the two natures of Christ. Because they carried over from Nicaea the antecedent conviction that Jesus and the Father shared one indivisible divine nature, they were forced to conclude that Jesus suffered his passion and death "according to the flesh," i.e., only in his human nature. This led then to the paradoxical conclusion that Jesus in his cry of abandonment on the cross ("My God, my God, why hast thou forsaken me?") was at one and the same time the one who abandoned and the one who was abandoned. In Mühlen's eyes, this speculative enigma only illustrates the bankruptcy of a prepersonal concept of God as divine substance, inherited from Greek philosophy, to explain the rich interpersonal relations of Father and Son, as given in Sacred Scripture. Hence at this point he is ready to depart from the terminology of the Church Fathers in order to work out a new understanding of the divine nature which will be at one and the same time faithful to Sacred Scripture and much more relevant to the changed world-consciousness of modern man/woman, referred to above.

This task carries him first into a re-examination of the celebrated text from Exodus in which Jahweh reveals his *name* to Moses. However one translates *ehjeh ašer ehjeh* (Ex. 3:14), it means, says Mühlen, God's promise of fidelity to his people. He is therefore pre-eminently a personal God who is abidingly with his people. His nature is unchanging, not in the sense of an indivisible divine substance as rather in terms of his constant fidelity to his promises. When Jesus in the New Testament, therefore, says, "The Father and I are one" (Jn. 10:30), he is presumably making reference not to the unity of the divine substance, as rather to the quality of the interpersonal relationship existing between himself and the Father. That is, if Jahweh is with his people, he is unquestionably with his Son in even more intimate fashion. Together they constitute a community (*Wir-Gemeinschaft*); and this, says Mühlen, is what is really meant by the conciliar statement that Jesus is homoousios, of the same reality, with the Father.[37]

If, however, the essence of God is to be a community, then, says Mühlen, the Holy Spirit is clearly the personification of the divine essence. That is, insofar as the Spirit has always been understood as the bond of union between the Father and the Son, he who constitutes community between the other two divine persons, then the Spirit is the communitarian reality of God in person. This is, of course, in keeping with Mühlen's earlier work on the Trinity, explained above. But, for fundamentally the same reasons as before, I have problems with this understanding of the role of the Spirit within the Trinity. The Spirit seems to be thereby depersonalized, subtly reduced to a *process* of interaction between the Father and the Son. I will reserve, however, further comment on this point, until after I have completed the exposition of Mühlen's thought.

In the fourth and final part of the work, Mühlen applies these new thoughts on the nature and essence of God to an understanding of the person of Christ, above all in his passion and death on the cross. Earlier, in interpreting Exodus 3:14, he had said that the unchanging character of God's nature was his unwavering fidelity to his people, his desire to be with them in all their trials and troubles. Specifying the nature of God still further, Mühlen now says that it consists in the giving away of one's own (*Weggabe des Eigensten*).[38] The Father, accordingly, possesses the divine nature in that he gives up his own Son for our salvation (Rm. 8:32); the Son is divine in that he allows himself to be thus delivered up for our salvation; finally, the Spirit shares in the divine nature, in that he is the personification of the process of self-giving within the Godhead. This process of self-giving culminated in Christ's passion, above all in his cry of abandonment from the cross. For at that moment the Father had given up his Son to a shameful death; the Son was experiencing his total abandonment by the Father; and yet the two of them were simultaneously reunited with one another through the Spirit who communicated to both of them this very same passion for self-giving. Hence the death of Jesus on the cross reveals the mystery of the inner life of God. God is the process of self-giving love; all three divine persons share in that process, although, as noted above, in different ways.

Mühlen goes on to say that Jesus in expiring breathes out the Spirit upon the world. The moment of Christ's death is therefore the temporal manifestation (*Zeitwerdung*) of the Spirit, just as the Incarnation was the temporal manifestation of the Son. The Spirit, once breathed forth, remains in the world, but above all in the Church, to lead us to Christ and then through Christ to the Father. Concretely, this means that whenever human beings are led to acts of self-giving love, they experience, consciously or unconsciously, the three divine persons. Their immediate perception is, to be sure, only of the Spirit as the spirit of self-giving love. But, insofar as they give of themselves to their fellow human beings in that same spirit, they grow in the likeness of Christ and thus draw near to the Father as the ultimate source of self-giving love. Every human community, but principally the Church, is thus a symbolic representation of the divine nature or essence, i.e., God as a community of three divine persons.[39]

Very little is explicitly said here by Mühlen about the *suffering* love of God, beyond the one remark that the giving up of the Son had to affect the Father in his own person. But when he describes the essence or nature of God in terms of self-giving love, Mühlen clearly implies that the love in question here is a suffering love. It is a love which concerns itself with the other and his/her welfare to the point of self-exhaustion. As Williams remarks, suffering in its most generic form is simply to be moved or influenced by another in his/her being and activity. Pain as such is not essential to suffering; one can experience compassion in sharing another's joy as well as his/her sorrow. The main point then, on which both Mühlen and Williams agree, is that God is not Pure Act or Subsistent Being as in classical metaphysics. For within this frame of reference it is very difficult to conceive of God as being in any way really affected by the actions of his creatures. Rather God is a community of three divine persons who are deeply involved both with one another and with their human creatures in the process of salvation, the redemption of the world. Does this imply change in God? If by change is meant the possibility of a dramatic reversal of attitude among the three divine persons toward one another or toward their rational creatures (e.g., a movement from love to hate), then clearly change within God is just as impossible for Mühlen and Williams as it has always been for thinkers in the classical tradition. But, if by change is meant a growth or development in the overall relationship of the divine persons with one another and, above all, with their rational creatures, then Mühlen and Williams would, by implication at least, be ready to admit change within God. For the whole brunt of their remarks, summarized above, has been to say that creation has made a difference to God as well as to us human beings. The three divine persons are in some sense more fully themselves as a result of the decision to create finite creatures capable of saying yes or no to the divine initiative. There is, in any event, an outlet for their self-giving love which the three divine persons would not have had, had they not chosen to become involved precisely in this way.

At this point, I would like to take up more in detail the question raised earlier about the possible depersonalizing of the Spirit within Mühlen's scheme. As mentioned above, Mühlen accepts the traditional understanding of the Spirit as the bond of love between the Father and the Son. Insofar as he likewise interprets the nature of God to be an act of self-giving love (*Weggabe des Eigensten*), then the Spirit would seem to be only the nature personified rather than a distinct divine person of equal stature and identity with the Father and the Son. A much simpler explanation would seem to be that the nature of God is this process of self-giving love, in virtue of which there exist three divine persons: Father, Son and Holy Spirit. Each is a separate "I"; each can address the other two persons as "Thou." Each serves as the bond of union between the other two. What makes them one God instead of three gods is the ongoing process of self-giving love which is their common nature. They constitute, in other words, a community, and this community of three divine persons is what we really mean by the generic term *God*.

I myself have developed this hypothesis in a pair of articles for the *Heythrop Journal* some years ago; in the next chapter, I will set forth the main lines of that proposal. But for the moment I simply wish to call attention to the fact that Mühlen and others like him seem to have shifted from a static, substance-oriented understanding of God to a more dynamic, process-oriented approach without thinking through all the consequences of that decision. Mühlen, as noted above, contends that the universe is no longer to be conceived as an impersonal Whole but rather as an interpersonal We. God too is to be considered a community of persons, at least with respect to the Father and the Son. The Spirit, however, appears to be a shadow personality, so to speak, merely the personification of the process which unites the Father and the Son. It might, of course, be counter-argued that unless the Spirit is the personification of the process, then there will be not three, but four, realities in God: namely, the three divine persons and the underlying divine nature conceived as a process of self-giving love. But, in line with process thought as developed by Whitehead and his followers, one could then respond that there is no real distinction between the persons and the process. The persons through their interaction with one another constitute the process of self-giving love and the process in turn "produces" the persons as the distinct individuals that they happen to be. Hence, very much in line with classical thought on the Trinity, "person" and "nature" are only rationally distinct from one another. The only difference is that by "nature" is meant, not the divine substance as in the classical approach, but rather the divine life, understood as an interpersonal process. Admittedly, within this context the traditional relationships of origin defining the separate "personality" of the three divine persons would have to be rethought and perhaps subordinated to more fundamental relationships of equality existing among the three divine persons as members of one and the same divine community. But the relationships of origin, after all, were conceived in terms of a substance-oriented model for the nature of God. If the transition is made to a process-oriented approach, then perhaps the relationships of origin will cease to be of such crucial importance for the understanding of the Trinity.

3
New Approaches
to the Trinity: II

Still another German theologian who has developed a doctrine of the Trinity quite similar to Mühlen is Eberhart Jüngel. In an early work, *Gottes Sein ist im Werden* (translated and published in the United States under the title *The Doctrine of the Trinity: God's Being is in Becoming*[40]), Jüngel presents a "paraphrase" of Karl Barth's doctrine of the Trinity, especially as given in the *Church Dogmatics*, in order to deal with the questions raised by Helmut Gollwitzer, in his book, *The Existence of God as Confessed by Faith*.[41] Gollwitzer had argued that God's being-for-us should not be allowed to overshadow his being-in-and-for-himself. For otherwise God's being-for-us would not be understood as the free gift which in fact it is. Jüngel counter-argues that Gollwitzer is still thinking in categories proper to the substance philosophy of Aristotle and not in the dynamic categories proper to an understanding of God based on the act of revelation (as in Barth's *Church Dogmatics*). He reasons thus: "God's being as subsistence is self-movement. As self-movement God's independent being makes revelation possible. Revelation as God's interpretation of himself is the expression of this self-movement of the being of God."[42] Hence the triple structure of God's self-revelation in his being-for-us, namely, as the revealing God and the event of revelation and its effect on man, is the copy (*Abbild*) of the original tripartite relationship of the persons of the Trinity among themselves. The Trinity is, accordingly, the attempt to think out the self-relatedness of God's being-in-and-for-itself.

Given this more dynamic frame of reference, Jüngel then takes up the crucial question of God's being as in becoming. He notes, first of all, that God's being is in becoming, not simply with respect to creation but from all eternity, in that Father, Son and Spirit by reason of a "primal decision" are already dynamically related to one another as a Trinity or three-in-one reality. They are, in a word, becoming ever more united with one another, even as each of them separately is becoming more distinctively himself. Furthermore, the intrinsic relatedness of the three divine persons to one another is the ontological ground of their becoming related to us, their rational creatures, without thereby becoming dependent on us for their being and activity. Yet, as noted above, the structure of God's self-communication in the act of revelation corresponds perfectly with the tripartite relationship of the persons to one another within the "immanent" Trinity. Through one and the same primal decision, therefore, the Second Person of the Trinity is both Son of God and Son of Man. Likewise, the Father is not related to the Son except in terms of the Son's further reality as Jesus, the revelation of God in history. Finally, in Jesus the Father can be said to suffer; i.e., he exposes himself to the threat of non-existence in the passion and death of Jesus. In the resurrection, to be sure, this threat of non-existence is definitively overcome, both for God in the person of Jesus and for all human beings united with Jesus in his passion and death. But, notes Jüngel, from still another perspective God's being is in becoming; in the passion, death and resurrection of Jesus, God (the Father) affirms himself anew as God, source of all being and life.

In a second book, published recently in Germany,[43] Jüngel expands on this "paraphrase" of Barth's doctrine in order to work out his own understanding of God, specifically, of God as revealed in the crucified Jesus. In the section of the book pertinent to our discussion, Jüngel begins by asking himself what is meant by the sentence "God is love" (1 Jn. 4:16). Genuine love, he says, is characterized both by selflessness (*Selbstlosigkeit*) and by self-relatedness (*Selbstbezogenheit*).[44] That is, in the act of loving, the self both gives itself away to the beloved and recovers its identity on another level as a free gift from the beloved. In true love, accordingly, there is involved a death to an older self in order to attain a new selfhood with the beloved; love is a dynamic unity of life and death for the sake of still richer and deeper life. Applied to God, this means, first of all, that God is necessarily triune. That is, if God loves himself, this means that there is in God one who loves (the Father), one who is loved (the Son), and the exchange of love between the Father and the Son (the Spirit). But, over and above this simple identification of persons within the Godhead, this means that God the Father is willing to sacrifice his pre-existing relationship with the Son, be separated from the Son in the latter's shameful death on the cross, in order to achieve a much deeper union with the Son (and through the Son with humankind as a whole) on another level. The Son in turn is willing to be given up for sinful human beings in order to achieve this deeper union with the Father and to bring his human brothers and sisters into the dynamic of self-giving love proper to the three divine persons in their relations with one another. Finally, the Spirit within this scheme is both the bond of love between Father and Son, reuniting them in the very moment of their separation from one another, and likewise the power of love at work in human minds and hearts to make those same human beings worthy of the Father's love.

To say that God is love, however, is not the same as to say that love is God. In Jüngel's opinion, this was the mistake of Ludwig Feuerbach who in his book, *The Essence of Christianity*, maintained that love is "divine" in that it brings human beings together but that the source of love is thus the interaction of men and women with one another rather than a transcendent God. Against this view, Jüngel argues that divine love, which is purely self-giving and never self-seeking, is qualitatively different from human love which is invariably a mixture of the two. Hence to affirm that God is love is to believe (a) that there is a transcendent source of human love and (b) that human love can be progressively transformed through contact with the divine. This contact with the divine is, of course, made possible in and through the life and, above all, the death of Jesus. Jesus was in his own person loving proof of the identity between God and self-giving love.

Self-giving love, however, implies the death of an older self in order to attain a new selfhood with the beloved. Applied to the Trinity, this means, as noted above, that the Father and the Son give up their pre-existing relationship with one another for the sake of sinful human beings, only to recover it on a deeper level in the very moment of Jesus' death on the cross. More specifically, how does this come about? First of all, says Jüngel, Jesus in his human consciousness could not think of himself except in terms of his relationship to the Father. Furthermore, in consequence of this self-surrender to the Father, Jesus enjoyed an unparalleled freedom in his dealings with his fellow human beings. He was able fearlessly to denounce the inequities of the Jewish Law, because he had no hidden ambition, no desire to promote self-interest at others' expense.

Eventually, this led him into conflict with the Scribes and Pharisees as the custodians both of the Law and of conventional wisdom. His shameful death on the cross, as one *according to the Law* cursed by God, was only the final act in Jesus' lifelong struggle to put love of God and one's neighbor ahead of the *pro forma* observance of the Law.

Granted that Jesus lived constantly in the immediate presence of the Father, nevertheless his death on the cross represented for him a moment of total abandonment by the Father. This, says Jüngel, is the striking paradox of the crucifixion; he who lived out his whole life in a spirit of self-surrender to the Father died as one abandoned to his fate by that same Father.[45] The Father too experienced a loss of his previous relationship with the Son when he witnessed Jesus' death on the cross. The separation between the two persons, Father and Son, was never so complete as in the moment of the crucifixion. Yet precisely in this moment of abandonment, the union between Father and Son was re-established in a deeper way by the Holy Spirit. The Spirit overcame the conflict between life and death in the relationship between Father and Son and thus grounded their union with one another on an even deeper basis: namely, that of self-giving love even unto death on a cross as a condemned criminal. The resurrection of Jesus is thus historical proof of the otherwise problematic belief that love is stronger than death or, as stated earlier, that love is the dynamic unity of life and death for the sake of richer and deeper life.

Explaining this latter idea at greater length, Jüngel suggests that love, both for God and for human beings, represents a growth or ascendancy (*Steigerung*) in one's being.[46] Quoting Matthew 10:39 ("Anyone who finds his life will lose it; anyone who loses his life for my sake will find it"), he maintains that true love is always characterized by the interplay of selflessness and self-relatedness within the consciousness of the lover. The more one gives of oneself, the more one grows in conscious self-possession. Applied to the Trinity, this means that Father and Son somehow enhance their previously existing relationship in virtue of the decision to give of themselves to their rational creatures: the Father through the gift of his Son to us, the Son through freely allowing himself to be given as such a gift. Yet on a deeper level the Father and Son remain more closely bound to one another than ever before. They have gained a new unity with one another through the activity of the Holy Spirit as the bond of love between them, the spirit of self-giving love.

Jüngel freely acknowledges that this understanding of the Trinity as grounded in the passion, death and resurrection of Jesus calls into question many of the traditional attributes of God, namely, his absoluteness, unchangeableness, imperviousness to suffering in any form, etc. But in his opinion, the ground for this new understanding of the

Trinity was laid long ago by Luther's Christolog and Hegel's philosophy. Furthermore, the Bible it self gives witness to God's involvement with hi people, his compassion for them in their trials an sufferings. Finally, argues Jüngel, one only play into the hands of atheists, if one continues to be lieve in an *apathetic* God, one who exhibits no con crete sense of concern for the fortunes of human beings in this life. What Jüngel does not mention here, but what clearly enters into his thinking on the matter, is his antecedent belief, already made clear in *The Doctrine of the Trinity*, that God's being is in process. A process approach to God logically de mands that the creation of the world and/or the re demption of the human race make a difference to the three divine persons, not only in their relations to us, their rational creatures, but also in their inner relationships to one another. A doctrine of the Trin ity, such as that produced by Jüngel, would thus seem to be virtually inevitable, once one begins thinking of God as a process of self-giving love rather than as the Pure Act of being.

Here, however, I must add the reservation, al ready mentioned in connection with the theory of Heribert Mühlen, about identifying the Holy Spirit with the process of self-giving love. It would be much more consistent with process thought, as I understand it, to identify the process with the divine nature and thus to free the Holy Spirit for some sort of personal identity equal to the other two divine persons. The three, in other words, could constitute a divine community, with each of the three persons playing a different role in the economy of salvation but with strict equality among themselves as regards their own inner life.

Many of these same thoughts are echoed in *Our Idea of God*, Volume Three in the five-volume *Theology for Artisans of a New Humanity* by Juan Luis Segundo, S.J. Segundo begins by calling attention to the fact that the current malaise in thinking or speaking about God is closely linked with our contemporary self-understanding both as individuals and as a race: "Our falsified and inauthentic ways of dealing with our fellow men are allied to our falsifications of the idea of God. Our unjust society and our perverted idea of God are in close and terrible alliance."[47] In justification of this hypothesis, Segundo first turns to the Bible, where he finds quite separate roles or functions within salvation history for each of the three divine persons. The Father is, for example, consistently represented as God before us in history. "From whatever viewpoint we look, God is the foundation we find already laid down for our destiny when we awaken to consciousness. Whatever direction we may give to our liberty, at its origin lies a world 'made by him,' a history started by his creative will."[48] Jesus, on the other hand, is God with us, he who shares our common human destiny and thereby inaugurates the ultimate in history. That is, the decisions of men and women since the time of Jesus are invested with special existential significance, since

they will inevitably contribute to or detract from the
Father's plan for the race, as manifested in the person and work of Jesus. Finally, the Spirit is God
within us, assuring the continuing presence of Jesus' word to human history in a creative way. All
three divine persons, accordingly, are intimately
linked to the ongoing process of history, the daily
struggle of human beings to make sense out of their
lives both as individuals and as a people.

Reflecting on the essence or nature of God thus
revealed in human history, Segundo concludes that
the three divine persons constitute a society. Their
nature is to be a community of three, and as such
they collaborate with one another in working out
our salvation. Jesus, for example, said: "The Father
and I are one" (Jn. 10:30). That is, between the
Father and Jesus there exists an I-Thou relationship
such that the two are "We," a community of persons. But Jesus could just as readily have said:
"The Spirit and I are one." For the Spirit is the
Spirit of Jesus himself, and in the Spirit Jesus is
present to his followers after his death and resurrection. Hence, says Segundo, it is only natural for us
to think of God as a community of three divine persons. Furthermore, it eliminates or at least reduces
a problem in human relations that has been caused
by the concept of God as absolute and self-sufficient. For, as long as God has thus been conceived as a being totally independent of his creatures, human beings have tended, subconsciously
perhaps, to imitate God in seeking their own self-

fulfilment in terms of self-sufficiency and independence of others. If, however, God is understood to
be a society of three persons who are sympatheti-
cally involved with men and women in history, then
human beings will perhaps recognize more readily
that they too have a basically social orientation, that
the perfection of their nature lies in interdepen-
dence with others for the achievement of common
goals, not in some unattainable ideal of independence and self-sufficiency.

Turning then to the two basic Trinitarian
heresies of the early Church, namely, Sabellianism
and Arianism, Segundo notes that these errors,
though officially condemned by the Church,
nevertheless subtly influenced the doctrine of God
in all subsequent centuries, even up to the present
day. The basic misconception of Sabellianism, for
example, was first the confusion of God with the
divine nature, and then the identification of the divine nature with eternal, unchanging, infinite being.
The (tri-)personal reality of God was thus hidden
behind an impersonal philosophical concept.
Moreover, this confusion between the abstract God
of the philosophers and the concrete God of
Judaeo-Christian revelation has lingered under
other forms in the minds of Christians ever since
and has subtly influenced their basic self-
understanding as human beings. Segundo gives one
example. In his mind, Christians have consistently
given a higher priority to the safe and sure attainment of the Good, namely, union with God as the

Supreme Good, than to the risk and creativity involved in the exercise of human liberty. Segundo quotes Blanche of Castile's remark to her son Louis, the future king of France and saint of the Church: "I would rather see you dead than have you commit one mortal sin." He then adds by way of commentary: "Blanche of Castile would prefer that her son, and *a fortiori* other human beings, opt for nonliberty rather than a specific use of liberty: i.e., choosing evil and that which is opposed to the law. And since one cannot attack a specific use of liberty without attacking it at its roots, i.e., without attacking liberty itself, she would simply prefer nonliberty."[49]

One might well question the universal validity of that last remark, but the general point being made by Segundo is quite clear and, to my mind, well taken. Because Christians have tended to think of God primarily, not as a personal being with free will, but rather as the Supreme Being, i.e., the universal principle of order and goodness in the world, they have seen human liberty more as a threat to the attainment of their already predetermined goal in life, namely, union with God in heaven, than as an opportunity for creativity and further personal growth. This in turn has prompted existentialist thinkers like Jean Paul Sartre to postulate the non-existence of God, so that man/woman can finally be free to work out his/her destiny in peace. A true Christian understanding of God as a society of free individuals who took upon themselves the risk of creation and redemption of the human race should, however, make Christians all the more aware of freedom as their most precious possession, a God-given gift to be used responsibly but, for that same reason, creatively in the service of others.

With respect to Arianism, Segundo notes that its basic misconception was an artificially severe distinction between the sacred and the secular, the religious and the profane. Arius could not believe in the dogma of the Incarnation, God truly become man, because he had antecedently accepted this absolute division between the divine and the human. Once again, says Segundo, this heresy was officially condemned by the Church, but its pernicious effects lingered on unnoticed in the subsequent teaching of the Church both about God and about man. For Christians continued to think of God as eternal and unchanging, the transcendent principle of a world order whose basic structure was fixed by divine decree. Hence God was implicitly associated with stability and permanence, in a word, adherence to the *status quo*, rather than with ongoing creative activity in the world. Christians, on the other hand, insofar as they sought to rethink basic principles and revise basic social structures immediately became suspect as enemies of the State, the Church, and ultimately of God himself. Here too, a proper Christian understanding of God as a society of divine persons actively involved in the process of human history would do much to free Christians psychologically for enthusiastic participation in the reconstruction of the social order. Contrarily, simplistic appeals by conservatively oriented individuals to natural law or the eternal order of things in order to block or at least retard the creative reinterpretation of the human condition and the restructuring of society would then be exposed for what they are: namely, the enduring legacy of the heresy of Arianism, the artificial separation of the sacred and the secular to the ultimate disadvantage of both.

Segundo's arguments here reflect his bias toward social activism as the best way to preach the Gospel at the present time. But his basic hypothesis that our falsified and inauthentic ways of dealing with our fellow men and women are closely allied to the traditional concept of God as absolute and self-sufficient is certainly thought-provoking. Likewise, his own counter-proposal that God should be understood as a society or community of divine persons finds confirmation in the reflections of Heribert Mühlen, who, as I mentioned earlier, would seem to be the most systematic of the thinkers covered thus far in Chapters Two and Three. Yet, with Segundo as with Mühlen, there remain certain philosophical questions which have to be answered before one can with confidence affirm that God is a society of persons. How does one, for example, avoid the charge of tritheism, that Father, Son and Spirit are in fact three gods with some loose affiliation with one another, but no real unity as one God? Is the notion of community such that it can constitute the nature or essence of God, the ontological basis for the unicity of God? Some years ago I wrote a pair of articles for the *Heythrop Journal* in which I tried to defend philosophically the hypothesis that God is a community of divine persons,[50] and it is to a summary of that argument that I now turn.

My model or paradigm for the understanding of community as such was drawn from the writings of the American philosopher Josiah Royce. In Part Two of *The Problem of Christianity*, Royce sketches a rudimentary metaphysics of community, beginning with the idea that "a true community is essentially the product of a time-process. A community has a past and will have a future. Its more or less conscious history, real or ideal, is a part of its very essence."[51] The community-building process, says Royce, is constituted by human beings engaged in acts of "interpretation" to one another. That is, they are seeking the truth about themselves, their relations to one another, the world of nature, the history of the universe, etc., through ongoing dialogue, continuous exchange of views on these same subjects. Thus each of the participants to the dialogue is himself/herself in process, continuously growing in knowledge of self, other human beings, the world, etc., and the interaction of these persons in process as individual beings constitutes the broader process which is the community. Moreover, the various communities of interpretation thereby established tend of their own inner dynamism, i.e., the search for an ever more

comprehensive grasp of the Truth, to merge with
one another and become still larger communities of
interpretation. In the final analysis, says Royce,
there both is and should be only one, all-
comprehensive Community of Interpretation, with
God himself directing the process as its chief interpreter. God, in other words, gives order and
direction to the cosmic process from within by sug-
gesting to his rational creatures the appropriate "interpretation" at any given moment. Whether or not
the human community ever attains that grasp of the
Truth which God already possesses as creator and
regulator of the process, it is in any case true that
"the history of the universe, the whole order of
time, is the history and the order and the expression
of this Universal Community" of interpretation.[52]

One could readily find fault with various details
of this metaphysical scheme, but what I found in-
triguing in trying to work out a new communitarian
interpretation of the Trinity was Royce's basic
hypothesis that individuals transcend themselves,
achieve a higher level of existence, in becoming
members of a community. As Royce himself saw
quite clearly, there are then "two profoundly different grades, or levels, of mental beings—namely,
the beings that we usually call human individuals,
and the beings that we call communities."[53] Communities, in other words, are specifically social
entities which constitute for their individual members a higher level of being and activity than would
be proper to them simply on the level of individual

existence. The communities cannot exist without their individual members, but the members cannot become fully themselves, achieve self-transcendence, until they participate in a community. Accepting Royce's basic insight here, I then further hypothesized in the articles referred to above that the Father, Son and Spirit are one God in virtue of their being a community of three divine persons. That is, none of them, taken singly, would be God; but only all three in dynamic interrelation with one another constitute one God. The nature of God therefore is to be a community of three persons. Without the individual persons there would surely be no community, but without the community, i.e., their dynamic interaction with one another, none of the three divine persons (nor all of them taken individually) would be God.

This represented, to be sure, an interpretation of Royce beyond his own expressed intentions. For, while he speaks of God in trinitarian terms in *The Problem of Christianity*, he apparently does not think of them as likewise a community. Rather they fulfill three separate but related functions vis-à-vis the human community. The Father is the transcendent deity, creator of the world process. The Son is identified with Jesus, the founder of the Church as the Beloved Community which over the centuries is meant to be the model for all other communities. The Spirit, finally, is the chief Interpreter of the Community, referred to above, who keeps the process of interpretation moving ahead in history under his personal supervision. But Royce himself apparently did not see that the apt counterpart to the Universal Community of humankind would be a transcendent divine community, with Jesus, so to speak, as the divinely appointed mediator between the two communities.

For my part, in writing those articles, I did not see as clearly then as I do now Royce's understanding of community as, in a word, *social* process, constituted by individuals who are on the level of individual existence likewise in process. For only if the members of the community are themselves mini-processes of basically the same structure and intentionality, can the community be considered a mega-process. Royce, admittedly, says that the dynamic of the process is based on cognition, not love. That is, his communities are communities of interpretation, not communities of self-giving love as such. But this is a minor point, above all, since Royce likewise lays heavy emphasis on loyalty to the community (in this sense, self-giving love) as the indispensable bond between members within the community. The far greater insight, to my mind, is his realization that the persons constitute the process and the process, in turn, constitutes the persons (at least as members of this particular community). Following that line of thought, I felt justified earlier in criticizing Mühlen and Jüngel for confusing the person of the Holy Spirit with the process of self-giving love common to all three divine persons. Identifying the Spirit exclusively with this process is, as I see it, to confuse "person" and "nature" within one's understanding of the Godhead.

One final area of research and reflection on the doctrine of the Trinity should be investigated before bringing this chapter to a close. In the Preface, I already made brief reference to Carl Jung's essay on the psychological meaning of the dogma of the Trinity.[54] His thought deserves further elaboration here, both because of the insights into our human experience of God therein contained and in view of subsequent developments in the area of Trinitarian theology. In his essay, Jung suggests that corresponding to the Father, Son and Spirit of classical Christian belief there are three archetypal ideas in the human psyche which have a profound effect on the religious experience of the individual. The "Father," for example, denotes "the earlier state of consciousness when one was still a child, still dependent on a definite, ready-made pattern of existence which is habitual and has the character of law. It is a passive, unreflecting condition, a mere awareness of what is given, without intellectual or moral judgment."[55] Within this stage of religious experience, God is invariably represented as an external authority-figure to whose laws or commands one submits without question. The "Son," on the other hand, is the symbol for the process of self-individuation within human beings, whereby the deeper personal reality which is the self asserts itself against the pattern of life imposed by the ego and reinforced by the customs of society. Jesus of

Nazareth, above all in his passion, death and resurrection, is the historical personage with whom the individual identifies in his/her struggle to achieve wholeness or integrity and thus to become with Jesus a God-like human being.[56] Finally, at the third level of religious consciousness, that of the "Spirit," the individual is prepared to give up his/her hardwon independence as an autonomous personality in favor of participation in some more comprehensive reality. "Spirit," accordingly, represents for human beings a return to the first stage of religious consciousness, but on a much more self-conscious and reflective level because of the process of individuation which took place in the intermediate stage (at the level of "Son"). Jung comments: "the advance to the third stage means something like a recognition of the unconscious, if not actual subordination to it."[57] The guide for one's life is no longer reason, discursive thought, but rather flashes of insight coming up from the unconscious and interpreted as the inspirations of the indwelling "Spirit."

Thus far Jung's reflections would be broadly compatible with classical Christian belief in the Trinity; the three archetypes make clear how Christian religious experience is (or at least should be) specifically Trinitarian. In the same essay, however, Jung goes on to propose that the symbol of the Trinity in human consciousness is ultimately to be replaced by a quaternity. To the "Father," "Son" and "Spirit" there must be added a fourth figure, namely, the "devil" who stands for the principle of evil in the world and is thus the dialectical opposite of Jesus as the "Son." Jung comments: "If God reveals his nature and takes on definite form as a man, then the opposites in him must fly apart: here good and there evil. So it was that the opposites latent in the Deity flew apart when the Son was begotten and manifested themselves in the struggle between Christ and the devil."[58] Human beings in the intermediate stage of religious consciousness are thus trapped in a violent struggle between the principles of good and evil (represented by Jesus and the devil) within themselves. Peace and a resolution of the conflict come only with the "Spirit," the third stage of religious consciousness in which, as Jung says, "God's love and God's terribleness come together in wordless union."[59]

Christian theologians have understandably been quite reluctant to accord any validity whatsoever to Jung's hypothesis of a quaternity in God.[60] For, quite apart from undermining the classical doctrine of the Trinity, it seems to grant to evil (whether personified as the devil or not) an objective reality and ontological status more in line with Gnosticism than Christianity. David Burrell, however, in a chapter of his recent book, *Exercises in Religious Understanding*, tries to come to terms with Jung on precisely this point. He, first of all, concedes that Jung has a point in saying that God is beyond good and evil in the ethical sense; as Aquinas also saw, God's goodness is based on his being, not on our human assessment of his actions toward us, his creatures.[61] Human beings too, in working through the process of individuation, transcend to some degree the ethical norms of good and evil; that is, whatever they have become in virtue of this process, is good (in an ontological sense) simply because it is. On the other hand, failure to cooperate with the process of individuation at work within oneself would be a classic instance of evil as a privation of good (*privatio boni*). By implication, then, God is good without admixture of evil because he is most perfectly himself; human beings, to the contrary, are a mixture of good and evil because they are not all that they can and should be. Turning to the notion of a quaternity in God, Burrell then suggests that this symbol can likewise be employed in the Christian understanding of God, if by the fourth member is meant, not the devil but the individual Christian and indeed the whole of humanity. In other words, this symbol is an apt representation of the process of salvation, whereby the individual believer and the race as a whole are incorporated into the Trinitarian life of God.

Here, however, I would offer a mild demur. It seems to me that this cosmological interpretation of the symbol of quaternity detracts from Jung's real insight into the subtle workings of the three divine persons within human consciousness. The triune God, in other words, becomes present to human beings psychologically in three fairly well-defined stages, corresponding to what Jung means by the "Father," the "Son" and the "Spirit." Furthermore, at the intermediate stage of the "Son," it is often not clear to the individual person how he/she should imitate Christ as the ideal self. The devil posing as an "angel of light" is a very real factor in the consciousness of the individual, as he/she tries to deal with the often conflicting demands of the ego and the self. Only from the perspective of the "Spirit" can one with relative assurance say that this or that decision is genuinely Christ-like and not the inspiration of the devil. Hence on this level of religious development, God will be experienced by the individual as the source of both good and evil, at least until he/she learns by experience to identify what is really good and what is truly evil. This says nothing, of course, about evil as a factor in God's own life. But Jung's intention with the symbol of the quaternity was clearly not to describe God as he exists in himself, but rather as he is experienced by human beings at various stages of their psychological and religious development.[62]

In Jung's mind, however, still another quaternity exists to supplement the traditional notion of God as triune: namely, the quaternity constituted by the Father, the Son, the Spirit and the Blessed Virgin Mary. As he sees it, the Roman Catholic belief in the bodily assumption of Mary into heaven is a tacit recognition of Mary's divinity and her rightful place within the God-symbol.[63] Earlier in his essay, Jung had dismissed the idea that the Holy Spirit could be interpreted as a mother-figure. For then the Christian Trinity would be indistinguish-

able from the "archaic family-picture" of ancien
polytheism, and the Spirit would lose his specia
function within the Godhead: "not only is he the lif
common to Father and Son, he is also the Paraclet
whom the Son left behind him, to procreate in ma
and bring forth works of divine parentage."[64] At th
same time, Jung freely admits that feminine imager
has been often used to describe the activity of th
Spirit within the soul of the believer. "Where judg
ments and flashes of insight are transmitted by un
conscious activity, they are often attributed to a
archetypal feminine figure, the anima or mother
beloved. It then seems as if the inspiration came
from the mother or from the beloved, the 'femm
inspiratrice.' "[65] These observations, combined
with his insistence on the quasi-divinity of the
Blessed Virgin Mary, would lead one to conclude
that Jung saw the need for a distinctively feminine
dimension within the God-symbol.

A recent book, written more in popular style
than according to scholarly canons, takes up anew
the hypothesis, initially rejected by Jung, that the
Holy Spirit should be understood as a feminine
principle within the Godhead.[66] The authoress,
Joan Schaupp, writes out of her personal experience and prayerful reflection on the Scriptures, especially the Wisdom literature of the Hebrew Bible.
Her conclusion is that she as a woman is in a special
way patterned after the Holy Spirit. That is, the
roles traditionally assigned to the Spirit in
Scripture, namely, breath of life, consoler, coun-

selor and helpmate, all fit the pattern of her life as wife and mother. Feminists, no doubt, would object that Schaupp is thereby indirectly confirming the stereotyped behavior-patterns of women in Western civilization, hence that she is unconsciously doing a disservice to the cause of women's liberation. Schaupp, however, defends her position with reference to Jung. Jung urged the recognition of both male and female characteristics in oneself as a part of integral personal development. Both men and women, however, have been hampered in this integration process by the image of an all-male God. Men have been embarrassed to admit the feminine side of their nature; women, on the contrary, have been all too aware of their femininity but ashamed to advocate it openly in a male-dominated society. What is needed, therefore, says Schaupp, is a recognition of the femininity of God, and this, following the lead of Scripture itself, is most aptly done by reflection on the person and role of the Holy Spirit in the economy of salvation.

Whatever scholars might think of Schaupp's exegesis of various texts from Scripture, it is clear that she has touched on a very significant issue for the contemporary understanding of God. Men and women are jointly made in the image and likeness of God (Gn. 1:27). Hence human sexuality, at least in its broader psychological implications, must somehow reflect the nature and reality of God. Yet, as Schaupp points out, the image of an all-male God has effectively repressed the latent femininity of

God and, by implication, the femininity of human nature, albeit in different ways for men and women. Something must be done, therefore, to restore the value of the distinctively feminine both to our understanding of God and to our self-understanding as human beings, whether men or women.

From the viewpoint of speculative theology, the biggest roadblock to a proper recognition of the feminine in God is surely the traditional relationships of origin used to describe the generation of the Son from the Father and the spiration of the Spirit from both the Father and the Son. Within such a scheme there is no natural place for a feminine principle. As we saw above, the Father-Mother-Son configuration was rejected by Jung, both because it reflected a more primitive polytheism and because it failed to highlight the distinctive role of the Spirit in the relation between the Father and the Son and in the economy of salvation. But, if one were to see the relationships of origin as just one of many possible relationships existing between three co-equal persons within the Godhead, if, in other words, the basic analogy for the Trinity was that of an interpersonal community rather than a family in some extended sense of the word, then the way might well be clear for an investigation of the feminine in God, as reflected not just in the Spirit, but in the Father and the Son as well. For example, perhaps the feminine in the Spirit is to be found in the way that she/he mediates between the Father and the Son, serves as the bond of love for the other two persons.

But by the same token, if one accepts the analogy of an interpersonal community for the understanding of the Trinity, the Father mediates between the Son and the Spirit, and the Son serves the same function for the relationship between the Father and the Spirit. Hence there is an undeniably feminine side to the "personalities" of the Father and the Son as well as of the Holy Spirit. In any case, the speculative possibilities are endless, once one breaks free of the traditional relationships of origin as the definitive mode of explanation for the connection of the persons with one another within the Trinity. The big question, of course, is whether one can and should take that step.

Epilogue: The Future of the Trinity

In his recent book, *The Becoming of the Church*, Bernard Lee suggests that there are two rival dynamics at work in the communitarian process called Church. The first is the survival dynamic which guarantees continuity with the past; the second is the intensity dynamic which generates relevance for the present.[67] Both dynamics are indispensable for the continued health and well-being of the Church community, even though they have opposite effects on the people involved and can thus co-exist within these same individuals only under conditions of stress and anxiety. In reviewing the preceding chapters in which such a variety of different theories on the Trinity were presented, one may feel perhaps within one's own person the stress arising from the interaction of these two dynamics. On the one hand, in conformity with the survival dynamic, one might look with alarm at some of the new approaches to the Trinity presented in Chapters Two and Three. The notion of the Trinity as interpersonal process, for example, so that the unity of the divine nature lies precisely in the community of the three divine persons with one another, possibly awakens the fear of tritheism. Similarly, the idea that the three divine persons genuinely suffer, are changed as a result of their relations with their human creatures, might well make one wonder whether God has not become all too human within the theories of some theologians. Finally, the still more bizarre concept of the femininity of God might be offensive to not a few. But, on the other hand, if belief in the Trinity is to be genuinely relevant to our present generation, it must be interpreted in terms appropriate to contemporary self-understanding. That is, human beings are more aware than ever before of the need for community, of the fact of change or development, often accompanied by deep suffering, in human life, and finally of the distinctively bisexual character of all human relations. If the concept of God, specifically of God as triune, does not in some way reflect these all-pervasive human concerns, then it will cease to be truly relevant to present-day men and women. The intensity dynamic within the Church, at least with respect to the key dogma of the Trinity, will have capitulated to the more urgent promptings of the survival dynamic; security in one's beliefs will be more highly valued than relevance to the contemporary scene.

It would be out of place for me at this point to suggest how others should resolve for themselves that conflict of interests in the matter of the Trinity. The whole purpose of a booklet like this is simply to put the reader in touch with contemporary theological reflection, let him/her, so to speak, see which way the wind is blowing. My own decision in this matter is, I think, indirectly reflected in the criticism which I offered to the various theories as they came up for review. I am, in other words, willing to rethink and recast the traditional understanding of the Trinity in the hope of eventually coming up with a concept of God as triune that genuinely speaks to modern-day men and women. On the other hand, I would insist that a processive, communitarian, bisexual approach to the Trinity be incorporated within a broader systematic frame of reference, so that the Trinity thus interpreted would be only one part, although perhaps the key part, in an overall reinterpretation of Christian dogma along processive, communitarian, bisexual lines. Only thus, it seems to me, is the very real danger of theological dilettantism in this matter of the Trinity laid aside. The classical doctrine of the Trinity was the crowning point of a very impressive philosophical and theological synthesis which embraced the totality of Christian doctrine. If there is to be a successor to the classical doctrine, then it can be proposed only on the basis of an equally comprehensive and rigorously systematic approach to theology.

Having said this, I would conclude by saying that I think process theology, among all the philosophical and theological constructs in vogue at the moment, offers the most exciting possibilities for a new synthesis of Christian doctrine. By process theology, however, I do not mean exclusively the philosophy of Alfred North Whitehead as adapted to a Christian context by one or other of his disciples. While there has been much good work done in this area by Hartshorne, Cobb, Lee, *et. al.*, I still have misgivings about the use of Whitehead's philosophy to describe process on a communitarian or strictly interpersonal level. For Whitehead's basic models are all infrahuman in their original scope and intention. Actual entities, for example, are fleeting moments in ongoing processes on various levels of being and activity, and it is only through their combination into "societies" of various configurations that they become persons and societies on the common sense level of explanation. Although disciples of Whitehead may quite well be able to adapt these concepts to an explanation of human behavior on the personal and societal levels, nevertheless it makes more sense to me to work with the categories of a process thinker who is specifically concerned with the interrelation of persons and communities. In this respect, I think that the work of Josiah Royce in *The Problem of Christianity* has been too little read and analyzed. Further elaboration on this point would, however, carry me beyond the scope of the present essay. Suffice it to say that process thought in some form or other seems to offer the best vehicle currently available for the systematic articulation of the various new insights on the Trinity contained in Chapters Two and Three above.

Notes

1. K. Rahner, *The Trinity* (New York, 1970), p. 10.
2. C. G. Jung, *Collected Works*, XI (*Psychology and Religion: West and East*), 109-200.
3. *Ibid.*, p. 113.
4. Thomas Aquinas, *Summa Theologiae*, I, QQ. 29-43.
5. B. J. F. Lonergan, S.J., *De Deo Trino*, 2 vols. (Rome, 1964): II, 186.
6. Rahner, *op. cit.*, pp. 32-33.
7. *Ibid.*, p. 36.
8. *Ibid.*, p. 106.
9. *Ibid.*, p. 38.
10. *Ibid.*, p. 106.
11. *Ibid.*, p. 54.
12. *Ibid.*, p. 56.
13. H. Mühlen, *Der heilige Geist als Person*, 2nd ed. (Münster, 1966), pp. 1-4; 11-16.
14. *Ibid.*, p. 56.
15. D. von Hildebrand, *Metaphysik der Gemeinschaft* (Regensburg, 1955), p. 34.
16. Mühlen, *op. cit.*, pp. 116-117. Cf. also E. Cousins, "A Theology of Interpersonal Relations," *Thought* XLV (1970), 56-82. This article gives an excellent summary and critique of Richard of St. Victor's approach to the Trinity.
17. Aquinas, *op. cit.*, I, Q. 36, a. 4, ad 7.
18. Mühlen, *op. cit.*, pp. 127-128. Cf. also pp. 2-3, where he notes that "person" as applied to the members of the Trinity can never signify an individual consciousness or subsistent center of operations.
19. J. Moltmann, *The Crucified God*, trans. R. Wilson & J. Bowden (New York, 1974), p. 207.
20. *Ibid.*, p. 243.

21. K. Barth, *Church Dogmatics*, II, 2 (Edinburgh, 1957), 163-168.

22. Moltmann, *op. cit.*, p. 246.

23. *Ibid.*, p. 253.

24. A. N. Whitehead, *Process and Reality* (New York, 1929), p. 529.

25. A. N. Whitehead, *Religion in the Making* (New York, 1926), p. 155.

26. L. Ford, "Process Trinitarianism," *Journal of the American Academy of Religion* XLIII (1975), 207.

27. D. D. Williams, *The Spirit and the Forms of Love* (New York, 1968), p. 126.

28. *Ibid.*, p. 121.

29. *Ibid.*, p. 162.

30. *Ibid.*, p. 166.

31. *Ibid.*, p. 183.

32. *Ibid.*, p. 167.

33. *Ibid.*, p. 185.

34. Whitehead, *op. cit.*, pp. 521-533.

35. H. Mühlen, *Die Veränderlichkeit Gottes als Horizont einer zukünftigen Christologie* (Münster, 1969).

36. *Ibid.*, p. 13.

37. *Ibid.*, pp. 22-23.

38. *Ibid.*, p. 31.

39. For further elaboration on this point, cf. R. Sears, S.J., "Trinitarian Love as Ground of the Church," *Theological Studies* XXXVII (1976), 652-679. Sears uses Mühlen's ideas in this essay as the basis for his own reflections.

40. Trans. H. Harris (Grand Rapids, Mich., 1976).

41. Trans. J. W. Leitch (Philadelphia, 1965).

42. Jüngel, *The Doctrine of the Trinity*, p. 93.

43. E. Jüngel, *Gott als Geheimnis der Welt. Zur Begründung der Theologie des Gekreuzigten im Streit zwischen Theismus und Atheismus* (Tübingen, 1977).

44. *Ibid.*, p. 435.

45. *Ibid.*, p. 495: "Die besondere Härte der Gottverlassenheit Jesu am Kreuz ist die Erfahrung der Gottverlassenheit im Horizont einer ganz von Gott sich beziehenden Existenz."

46. *Ibid.*, p. 505.

47. J. L. Segundo, S.J., *Our Idea of God* (Maryknoll, N.Y., 1974), pp. 7-8.

48. *Ibid.*, p. 22.

49. *Ibid.*, p. 108.

50. J. Bracken, S.J., "The Holy Trinity as a Community of Divine Persons," *Heythrop Journal* XV (1974), 166-182; 257-270.

51. J. Royce, *The Problem of Christianity*, 2nd ed. (Chicago, 1968), p. 243.

52. *Ibid.*, pp. 340-341.

53. *Ibid.*, p. 122.

54. Cf. above pp. 1-2.

55. Jung, *op. cit.*, p. 181.

56. Cf. on this point the recent book by Sebastian Moore, *The Crucified Jesus Is No Stranger* (New York, 1977).

57. Jung, *op. cit.*, p. 183.

58. *Ibid.*, p. 175.

59. *Ibid.*, p. 176.

60. Cf. J. W. Heisig, "Jung and Theology: A Bibliographical Essay," *Spring: An Annual of Archetypal Psychology and Jungian Thought*, 1973, 219-221.

61. D. Burrell, C.S.C., *Exercises in Religious Understanding* (Notre Dame, Ind., 1974), pp. 226-227; also 106-113.

62. Not everyone, of course, agrees with this benign interpretation of Jung's intentions in the essay. Cf., for example, R. Hostie, S.J., *Religion and the Psychology of Jung*, trans. G. R. Lamb (New York, 1957), pp. 198-210; likewise W. J. Hill, O.P., "Religious Understanding: Running through Burrell's 'Exercises,'" *The Journal of Religion* LVII (1977), 181-182.

63. Jung, *op. cit.*, pp. 170-171. Cf. also "Answer to Job," *op. cit.*, pp. 461-469.

64. *Ibid.*, p. 159.

65. *Ibid.*, p. 161.

66. J. Schaupp, *Woman: Image of the Holy Spirit* (Denville, N.J., 1975).

67. B. Lee, S.M., *The Becoming of the Church. A Process Theology of the Structures of Christian Experience* (New York, 1974), pp. 196-200.

Bibliography

(This list is consciously limited to books and articles on the Trinity in English. For those able to read French, German and other modern European languages, cf. the bibliography published by *Ephemerides Theologicae Louvanienses* under the topic "de Trinitate" for the past few years.)

BOOKS

Fortman, Edward J., *The Triune God. A Historical Study of the Doctrine of the Trinity* (Philadelphia, 1972).

Hodgson, Leonard, *The Doctrine of the Trinity* (London, 1944).

Jüngel, Eberhard, *The Doctrine of the Trinity. God's Being Is in Becoming* (Grand Rapids, Mich., 1976).

Moltmann, Jürgen, *The Crucified God* (New York, 1974).

Panikkar, Raimundo, *The Trinity and the Religious Experience of Man* (Maryknoll, N.Y., 1973).

Rahner, Karl, *The Trinity* (New York, 1970).

Segundo, Juan Luis, *Our Idea of God* (Maryknoll, N.Y., 1974).

Welch, Claude, *In This Name. The Doctrine of the Trinity in Contemporary Theology* (New York, 1952).

ARTICLES

Bracken, Joseph, "The Holy Trinity as a Community of Divine Persons," *Heythrop Journal* XV (1974), 166-182; 257-270.

Braine, David, "Observations on the Trinity: A Response to Professor Lockman," *Theology* LXXVIII (1975), 184-190.

Carmody, John, "Lonergan on the Divine Missions," *Laval Théologique et Philosophique* XXX (1974), 315-332.

Cousins, Ewert, "A Theology of Interpersonal Relations," *Thought* XLV (1970), 56-82.

Ford, Lewis, "Process Trinitarianism," *Journal of the American Academy of Religion* XLIII (1975), 199-213.

Hasker, William, "Tri-Unity," *Journal of Religion* L (1970), 1-32.

Hill, Edmund, "Our Knowledge of the Trinity," *Scottish Journal of Theology* XXVII (1974), 1-11.

Hill, William, "Does the World Make a Difference to God," *The Thomist* XXXVIII (1974), 146-164.

Jung, C. G., "A Psychological Approach to the

Dogma of the Trinity," *Collected Works* XI (*Psychology and Religion: West and East*), 109-200.

Jüngel, Eberhard, "The Relationship between 'Economic' and 'Immanent' Trinity," *Theology Digest* XXIV (1976), 179-184.

Kaiser, Christopher, "The Discernment of Tri-unity," *Scottish Journal of Theology* XXVIII (1975), 449-460.

————, "The Ontological Trinity in the Context of Historical Religion," *Scottish Journal of Theology* XXIX (1976), 301-310.

Kelly, Anthony, "Trinity and Process: Relevance of the Basic Christian Confession of God," *Theological Studies* XXXI (1970), 393-414.

Kress, Robert, "The Church as *Communio*: Trinity and Incarnation as the Foundations of Ecclesiology," *The Jurist* XXXVI (1976), 127-158.

Lehmann, Paul, "The Tri-unity of God," *Union Seminary Quarterly Review* XXI (1965), 35-49.

Lockman, Jan, "The Trinity and Human Life," *Theology* LXXVIII (1975), 173-183.

Meynell, Hugo, "The Holy Trinity and the Corrupted Consciousness," *Theology* LXXIX (1976), 143-151.

Pittenger, Norman, "Trinity and Process: Some Comments in Reply," *Theological Studies* XXXII (1971), 290-296.

Schoonenberg, Piet, "Process or History in God," *Theology Digest* XXIII (1975), 38-44.

————, "Trinity—The Consummated Covenant: Theses on the Doctrine of the Trinitarian God," *Studies in Religion* V (1975-1976), 111-116.

Sears, Robert, "Trinitarian Love as Ground of the Church," *Theological Studies* XXXVII (1976), 652-679.

Spicer, Malcolm, "The Trinity: A Psychological God," *Studies in Religion* V (1975-1976), 117-133.

Torrance, Thomas, "Toward an Ecumenical Consensus on the Trinity," *Theologische Zeitschrift* XXXI (1975), 337-350.